THE MIST GRILL

THE MIST GRILL

rustic cooking from Vermont

STEPHEN SCHIMOLER

with photographs by Peter Miller

INVISIBLE CITIES PRESS
MONTPELIER, VERMONT

Invisible Cities Press
50 State Street
Montpelier, VT 05602
www.invisiblecitiespress.com

Library of Congress Cataloging-in-Publication Data

Schimoler, Stephen G.
The Mist Grill : rustic cooking from Vermont / Stephen G. Schimoler.
p. cm.
Includes index.
Cloth ISBN: 1-931229-03-1
Paper ISBN: 1-931229-21-x
1. Cookery, American. 2. Cookery—Vermont. I. Mist Grill (Restaurant) II. Title.

TX715 .S1453 2001
641.5'09743—dc21
2001042437

Manufactured in the United States

Book design by
Peter Holm
Sterling Hill Productions

FIRST EDITION

For Robin, "The Great Enabler and Inspirer," who has been unwavering in her understanding, support, passion, and patience with me! And to my children, Stevie and Kirsten, who have been on the short end of the sacrifices I have made in my life pursuing this career.

ACKNOWLEDGMENTS

I'd like to thank all the people in my life who have supported my goals and my vision as a chef. Literally thousands of people—friends, family, and strangers— have been a part of my many food enterprises, from my parents, children, and partners to the cooks, chefs, and other restaurant personnel I've worked with— such as José, who landed from El Salvador and washed dishes, prepped, cooked, schlepped, and performed every conceivable job in my restaurants for eight years. Succeeding in the kitchen requires intense commitment to hard work and a passion to create. It is that passion, shared with mentors, coworkers, and compatriots, that has shaped my career. To all of you, thanks for the fire!

Special thanks to my closest supporters: Robin Schempp, my partner in everything; my parents, "Doc" and Bea; Stevie and Kirsten Schimoler; Graham Kerr, Julia Child, Dave Burke, Todd English and Doug Rodriquez, Stefan Kappes, Jeff Lawton, John Redmond, Ken Vanderpoel, Mim Pearl, Rob Messinger, Invisible Cites Press, and all the characters who know I should have mentioned them:

Thank you!

CONTENTS

Introduction / 1

It's About the Food / 4
The Pantry / 6
The History of the Mill and Grill / 7

Little Surprises / 11

Cherry Tomatoes with Goat Cheese, Cracked Pepper, and Honey Drizzle / 15
Vegetable Spoon Explosions / 16
Crab and Caviar Bomblets / 17
Oven-Roasted Balsamic Olives / 18
Savory Palmiers with English Mustard / 19
Tomato-Poached Shrimp / 20
Mini Grilled Polenta Sandwich / 21

Leafy Things / 23

Mist Greens with Robin's Sherry Vinaigrette / 27
Shaved Fennel and Parmesan with Prosciutto and Blood Orange Vinaigrette / 28
Warm Spinach with Pan-Roasted Pears, Stilton, and Cranberry Vinaigrette / 29
Bibb Lettuces with Roasted Red Pepper Dressing, Toasted Pistachios, and Goat Cheese / 30
The Steak House Wedge / 32
Summer Tomatoes with Arugula, Steve's Spiced Pecans, and Balsamic Vinaigrette / 33

Small Plates / 35

Warm Stilton Flan with Grilled Pears and Brown Bread / 39
Smoked Trout Cakes with Horseradish Crème Fraîche / 41
Grilled Shrimp on Creamy Grits with Tomato Chili Puree / 43
Capellini alla Black Walnut / 45
Thai Peanut Butter and Jelly with Mesclun and Orange Soy Dressing / 46
Purple Potato *Causa* Topped with Pulled Chicken and Balsamic Vinaigrette / 48
Salmon and Tuna Sashimi Towers with Wasabi Cream and Sesame Oil / 50
Tomato-Mozzarella Club with Basil and Balsamic Syrup / 51

Wild Mushroom and Goat Cheese Tartlets / 52
Doug's Coconut Tuna Ceviche / 54
Oven-Roasted Portabella with Corn and Roasted Garlic Flan / 55

Sides, Spuds, Soups, and Stuff / 59

Killer Rösti Potatoes / 63
Aged Cheddar and Heavy Cream Grits / 64
Pan-Mashed Potatoes / 65
Tomato Confit / 66
Risotto Cakes with Asiago Gratin / 67
Smoky and Spicy Black Beans / 68
Bea's Firecracker Apple Fritters / 69
Grilled Ratatouille / 70
Israeli Couscous Risotto-Style / 71
Lobster Latté / 72
Cream of Portabella / 74
Mushroom Cappuccino / 75
Corn Chowder with Shrimp and Green Chilies / 76
Roasted Tomato, White Bean, and Spinach Soup / 77
Creamy Chipotle Polenta / 78
Summer Fair "Dipped" Corn on the Cob / 79
Robin's "I Invented It" Mac and Cheese / 80
Summer Pea Salad / 81
Thai Coleslaw / 82
Steve's Red Spud Salad with Dijon Dressing / 83

Big Plates / 85

Sea Salt and Sage Crusted Chicken with Pearl Onion Gravy and Robin's Mac and Cheese / 89
Oven-Roasted Cod with Clam Chowder Broth / 90
Grilled Ribeye of Beef with Blue Cheese Butter and Tomato Cruda / 91
Dave Burke's Roasted Pork Shank with Poppy Seed Kraut / 93
Black Cherry and Chipotle Baby Back Ribs / 94
Grilled Yellowfin Tuna with Summer Tomato Cruda / 95
Pan-Roasted Monkfish with Lobster Stock and Barley / 96
Roasted Half Duck with Marinated Apricots and Lingonberry Demiglace / 98
Jason's Apple Crisp Salmon with Wilted Greens and Reduced Cider / 100
Dijon-Crusted Rack of Lamb / 101
Mushroom Tarte Tatin with Parmesan Anglaise and Truffle Oil / 102
Maple-Glazed Oven-Roasted Chicken with Grilled Apple Hash / 103
Shrimp Churascaritas with Cilantro Chimichurri à la Kirsten / 104

Stevie's Alfredo Carbonara / 106
Chicken Saltimboca "Sinatra" / 107
Summer Vegetable and Portabella Napoleon / 108
Shrimp Tarte Tatin with Roasted Tomatoes and Calamata Olives / 109
Grilled Veal Chop with Wild Mushroom Ragout and Truffled Demiglace / 110

Sweet Rewards / 113

Vermont Maple Crème Brûlée / 117
Pear and Ginger Tarte Tatin with Allspice Anglaise / 118
Gingerbread Bomb / 120
Chocolate Almond Torte / 122
Lemon Curd Sandwich with Berry Sauce / 123
Apple and Bourbon Bread Pudding / 125
Peach and Basil Ice Cream / 126
Summer Fruit Strudel / 127
Open Apple Croustade with Cinnamon Cream / 128
Apple Crisp Pie with Sharp Cheddar / 129
Apple Cider and Dried Cranberry Granita / 130

The Grape and the Bean / 133

The Basic Comforts / 139

Blush Hill Pot Roast / 143
Slow Roast Chicken / 144
Boiled Dinner / 145
The Ploughman's Lunch / 146
One-Pan Pasta Rustica / 147
Sunday Morning Sante Fe Frittata / 148
Roast Leg of Lamb / 149
Stevie and Kirsten's Carmelized Apple French Toast / 150
Balsamic Vinaigrette / 151

Stocks and Crusts / 153

Veal Stock / 157
Chicken Stock / 159
Pie Crust / 160

Index / 161

INTRODUCTION

When you grow up, as I did, eating at a dinner table sometimes crowded with twelve hungry souls at a time, you soon realize that food not only provides necessary sustenance but also weaves through our lives a common thread of social experience. We six children ate very well, and we learned quickly that meals could be a cause for celebration every day of the year. I've always been intrigued by the social experience that surrounds food and cooking; that's what eventually led me to become a chef. I've been lucky enough to work with and under some wonderfully creative culinarians, but the most significant influence comes from growing up in a family that loved to eat.

In the simple times of the 1960s we enjoyed uncomplicated, straightforward, and unpretentious foods. My mother was an expert in turning out soul-satisfying versions of the great American comfort foods: succulent rib roasts, crispy fried chicken, baked potatoes dotted with yellow pools of melted butter, slabs of meat loaf served with freshly picked ears of corn, sweet icebox cakes, and the always reliable Jell-O mold. Yesterday, those dishes were considered fairly standard fare. Today, you might expect to pay $20 for any one of them in a trendy restaurant. What was once common has now become cutting edge. Why? Perhaps because the simple, rustic cookery represented by these old American standbys has never lost its appeal, despite changing tastes.

What do I mean by rustic cookery? In the dictionary *rustic* is defined as: "1—Typical of country life. 2—Simple, unsophisticated, bucolic." That's how I think of the recipes in this book and the dishes I serve at the Mist Grill— simple foods, prepared in a way that doesn't muddle the flavors or fuss with the presentation, but highlights the best country living has to offer. To me this is the essence of cooking! Over the years I've cooked in many kitchens and fed hundreds of thousands of people. In all the places I've cooked, I've relied on the quality of the ingredients and an approach that owed less to technical culinary training and more to inspiration. Not having attended a culinary school, I always cooked with an intuitive hand. Through this approach to food, I've been able to develop a simple style and method of cooking that reflect both the essential goodness of the foods of my childhood and the pace of country living.

When life led me to Vermont in 1990, my growing awareness of a simpler lifestyle heightened my desire to open a restaurant that could offer truly rustic food, yet also serve as a canvas for creativity and innovation. The Mist Grill has become that place.

Where once Vermont farmers brought their corn and wheat for milling, they now bring me their superb fruits and vegetables, which provide the backbone of the dishes we serve. The former gristmill, dating to 1807, has been resurrected as a place where the pace and currents of rural living are respected. We've reestablished the old mill's originally intended use, as a place where raw ingredients are refined to the point that they're suitable for consumption. Granted, we aren't serving our customers raw cornmeal; today it's polenta with Stilton cheese or steel-cut oats cooked with apricots and topped with maple syrup. But you get the idea.

The Mist Grill: Rustic Cooking from Vermont is a compilation of dishes we now serve, dishes that reflect simpler times yet are respectfully adapted for contemporary tastes with our signature style. We think they're hearty, simple, yet elegant dishes, bold in their flavors and, yes, rustic!

Rustic cooking can be many things, and its definition is certainly open for interpretation. But the common denominator might be a reliance on great ingredients that are not overly manipulated; instead they're allowed to speak for themselves in all their natural goodness. When a dish comes together there's a sense of comfort in knowing that the ingredients are still close to their origins. Rusticity, really, is as much a state of mind as it is a style of cuisine. So enjoy the experience!

It's About the Food

I believe that the most important ingredient in any recipe is passion! Without the desire to embrace the ingredients, the results can lack that special touch that makes a dish lodge in your memory bank. In the movie *Like Water for Chocolate,* a cook's emotions could be infused into food; unwitting diners ingested and shared the pain, sensuality, or love that the cook was feeling. That sort of passion is something to strive for.

There is some truth to the transforming power of meals, and the most powerful emotion that can be recognized when you present a plate in front of someone is, I think, passion. The level of care that compels cooks to add that little extra touch of color or flavor, slice the tomato paper thin, or made a stock from scratch reveals their passion and love.

It's also important to be passionate when procuring ingredients. For me, seeing and touching pristine ingredients such as a glistening bluefin tuna is almost a religious experience; there's no other color in the natural spectrum like fresh bluefin. Gently plucking a perfectly ripe tomato that's 80 degrees to the touch from the sun's warmth reflecting on its ruby skin, or feeling the sweet milky spray from a cob of corn as you shuck it just before plunging it into a waiting pot on a hot August evening; these can be transforming experiences for a cook. The intoxicating aroma of a basket of just-foraged morel mushrooms sitting on the kitchen counter, or the perfect simplicity of an egg and its diverse uses: these are my passions.

I have a favorite saying: "Oxygen, water, sex, and food; everything else in life is a bonus." Living without these things is impossible, and yet the preparation of our food is the only one that we can truly control and enjoy on our own terms. Food also provides an experience that for some can be more rewarding than sex!

My goal in writing this cookbook is to share some of the recipes that have been enjoyed by the thousands of patrons at the Mist Grill and to provide a guide to the approach and preparation you can use to achieve great results. I appreciate the effort that goes into capturing the precise measures and techniques found in most cookbooks, but I also feel strongly that no one reproduces a dish the same way every time. Using your intuition in the interpretation of a recipe is more rewarding, and will usually produce dishes that are more in keeping with your own style. People often tell me how intimidated they are by some cookbooks; the pressure to reproduce what they see in a photograph causes them not to even experiment with the dish. Being sensitive to these issues, I suggest that you use a cookbook as a guide more than a blueprint that must be followed to the letter. Even an accomplished chef can have difficulty reproducing someone else's recipe.

The food and recipes in *Mist Grill* are designed to allow for interpretation and employ convenient shortcuts or prepared ingredients that can save hours of time. There are so many great new products out there to use in place of home-made versions that—given our current time-compressed lifestyles—you should feel no guilt in trying them. I love to make scratch veal stock, going through the entire process of reducing, straining, reducing again, and getting a rewarding demiglace, but I'm the first to admit that I don't always have the time to do it. Yet it's a critical ingredient in many dishes and sauces. There are numerous commercial stocks, however, that are outstanding; they can be better and more consistent than what I make myself, and they're easy to customize. When these are only a component of the dish, and the other ingredients are of excellent quality and prepared correctly, the commercial foods you elect to use simply enhance the stars of the show!

The Mist Grill style of rustic cooking incorporates shades of imperfection as part of the formula. Onions that are diced too uniformly look contrived, tart shells that are too perfect can look fake, and julienned peppers identical in size sometimes look like they were cloned. Flavor is what we ultimately enjoy in a dish, and great flavors can be achieved without being overly fussy and pretty. Remember that cooking should be fun and rewarding to yourself and the recipients of your efforts.

The Pantry

Eating well starts with quality ingredients; I don't mean exotic or expensive, but ingredients at the peak of their flavor and freshness. In the Mist Grill kitchen we take for granted that our refrigerators and shelves are lined with everything we might need to complete a dish as we're cooking it. If quality ingredients are a start, then good preparation is probably half the battle. Having the right tools in your belt allows you to focus on the job at hand rather than agonizing over it. It's true, there are times where we don't have enough of a particular ingredient on hand, and it's these occasions when we improvise, slightly modifying the dish. This can be either good or bad, depending on the final outcome: bad if the dish suffers noticeably from the lack of a key ingredient, good if we've been forced to try something unusual that turns out to be exciting. Some great dishes and products were discovered over the years through this type of improvisation. It takes some folks years to be develop and tap taste memory banks to anticipate how a combination of flavors will work, but with experimentation and an arsenal of great foodstuffs, such a level of intuition and confidence can be attained.

But it is frustrating, when cooking from books, to read a recipe and realize that half the ingredients are difficult to find. In an effort to eliminate failed shopping trips, we at the Mist Grill have created a specialty products service designed to provide a wide assortment of those difficult- or impossible-to-find ingredients. ChefEx.net is a place for both home cooks and professionals to shop. The products are packaged in sizes that are sensible for all cooks and are delivered to your door. For instance, in many of the recipes in this book I suggest using chicken stock, veal stock, or demiglace. There are recipes for these stocks, but I'm the first to admit that at the Mist Grill we use the commercially prepared versions instead of making them from scratch—and we're certainly not alone in the restaurant world! So do what most fine restaurants do, get your demiglace from a commercial provider, and save yourself hours of work. If you're lucky enough to live near a great gourmet store, you can probably already find everything you need. But even then, we're able to provide versions of many products at a fraction of the retail cost. Check us out.

As I've already said, great dishes demand great ingredients. Still, even if you buy the freshest asparagus, if you overcook it, the quality is wasted. On the other hand, it's important not to waste good ingredients. The best olive oil may be essential to a superior vinaigrette, but not to sauté with. My point: You don't always need the best of the best for everyday use. Certainly when you're buying fish, meats, and produce the quality is important. The difference, for instance, between prime and choice cuts of beef is very noticeable, and the difference between good and bad fish—well, I don't think I need to tell you that! At the Mist Grill we pride ourselves on searching for great ingredients, and we rely on many of Vermont's boutique producers and growers for the rural, handmade, and hand-grown products we use. As the seasons change, we also tailor our menus to reflect available ingredients—spring mushrooms, summer tomatoes, autumn squash.

Unfortunately the summers are very short in Vermont; we never seem to have enough time to enjoy the full harvest of locally grown products. While they are available, though, we're in heaven! Each American region has its own special network of growers, and I encourage you to take advantage of the farmers' markets that pop up and to challenge your grocer to provide better cuts of meat or selections of fresh—not previously frozen—fish. If you're willing to pay a little extra for something special, make sure that it really is. Keep the pantry stocked (within reason), and don't hesitate to buy a product you've never tried before; you won't know what you like unless you try it!

The History of the Mill and Grill

The original Grist Mill in Waterbury, Vermont, first saw duty in 1807, milling local grains and corn for a backwoods community. Located on Thatcher Brook Falls, the Grist Mill employed the latest technology of its time, harvesting the energy from the powerful nearby waterfall to turn a network of gears, pulleys, and drive shafts that moved a huge stone wheel to crush wheat, rye, and corn. Sometime around 1840 the Mill was refurbished with a more modern works and outfitted with a new brick structure that stands today. (Our restaurant's dining room is located in the mill room with the original foundation from 1807.) The wall is lined with enormous stones, up to eight feet long and weighing more than a ton, and the workmanship amazes even the most jaded builders, designers, and architects.

The mill operated as a processor until 1938, and the building survived as a thriving feed store known as the Waterbury Feed Co. (The whitewashed letters are still visible on the building's facade, and we adopted it as our official corporate name.) The feed store closed in 1962 after the nearby interstate opened, and the building sat empty for more than thirty years, vandalized and subject to the rough elements of northern New England.

I had visited the town of Waterbury in late 1989, on my way to meet with Vermont's best-known ice-cream entrepreneurs, Ben and Jerry. I was still running food businesses in Long Island, and trying to get a line of flavored butters produced by the ice-cream guys. Following the meeting with Ben and Jerry, I took off to explore the area. Almost as soon as I got in the car, I noticed an abandoned building and pulled over to take a look. I'm a sucker for historic buildings, and so I walked around, peering through cracked windows and boarded-up doors. I saw the spectacular waterfall near the building and told myself that if I were ever to open a restaurant in Vermont, this would be the place. As I walked back to the car, I noticed a sign on the building and thought it read, "The Mist Grill." What a great name for a restaurant, I thought. The sign actually said "The Grist Mill," but I'd inadvertently transposed the letters. Eventually I found another Vermont dairy company (Cabot Creamery) to make my butters, and I moved my family to Waterbury.

For years, each time I drove past the abandoned mill, I envisioned my dream restaurant. But I always kept driving.

One evening during a dinner party, a friend announced he was going to open a new coffee-testing company in the old grist mill and that someone was going to open a restaurant there as well. My heart stopped; when I recovered, I told my guests the story of my vision for the mill. We began to discuss the fantasy of opening up a place together. We called the woman who owned the building. She said that the restaurant deal had fallen through the day before; it seemed like serendipity.

We arrived the next morning armed with legal pads and measuring tapes and started exploring the nooks and crannies of the old mill. It was clear that the place had enormous potential, but that it also would require an immense amount of hard work and financing to bring our vision to fruition. No heat, electricity, or plumbing had ever been installed, and the building was a shambles. The mill room was filled to the rafters with debris, and 150 years worth of spent grain hulls and petrified corncobs covered a dirt floor. In spite of all that, we looked past the debris and saw the great potential before us. The rock walls captivated us and we envisioned them lined with candles, diners filling the historic room. After crawling around for several hours and sketching pages of potential floor plans and concepts, we went our separate ways to ponder the possibilities.

More than six months passed while we worked out the details and created a partnership. While working on the restaurant's concept, we decided to include a bakery, a gallery and meeting space, and a café, as well as the coffee lab where all the coffee for the café and bakery would be roasted. We dove in and started the renovation.

We wanted to use as much of the existing materials and structure as possible, to honor the history each piece held, but we also wanted to introduce enough contemporary components to make the space reflect the innovation we intended to display through our dishes. The balance had to be perfect; otherwise, we might end up looking too touristy or as if we had abandoned the value of the old mill and its history. By using key structural elements and parts of the old millworks we were able to find that balance. Two massive timbers that once served as the footings for the millstone now do new duty as banquet benches. Much of the original ironwork has been transformed into railings. The result conveys the rustic history of the mill and also blends in new colors and textures that make every corner special and exude a welcome feeling to our diners. Looking back at the project, we wouldn't change a thing.

Diners who come to the Mist Grill immediately sense the deep history of the place and the reverence for the best of both old and new that makes the restaurant unique. We've tried to convey as much of this feeling as possible in this book, through the design, recipes, and photographs, but if a picture is worth a thousand words, an actual visit is worth a million—so you'll just have to make the trip to see for yourself.

LITTLE SURPRISES

For years I've tried to create a menu with dishes that serve as either simple hors d'oeuvres or meal starters that bring a little burst of flavor to tease the palate for what's to follow. The French call them *amuse bouche,* but I call them little surprises. During my years in the catering business, I learned to detest hors d'oeuvres: They meant immense amounts of work and a painstaking level of detail. Something that sounds simple, such as roast duck in mini pitas, can be a nightmare if you need to make a thousand of them for a party, among other selections.

Over the years I learned to create a number of little surprises designed to be attractive, flavorful, and, most important for me, really fast and easy to make. The secret is that "less can be more," especially when the dishes use few ingredients and can be assembled virtually to order. The beauty of these little surprises is that they can be served as passed or stationary hors d'oeuvres or placed on miniature plates, saucers, teacups, artistic glasses, slate roof tiles, or a multitude of other creative "plates," all of which help impart a sense of whimsy.

The recipes for these little surprises can be played with at your desire; they're easy to customize with a new garnish, touch of an herb or spice, a different cheese, or drizzle of a cool sauce or dressing. Enjoy the simplicity of these surprises and the power of the impression they'll make when you serve them up in some unique, fashionable way!

Cherry Tomatoes with Goat Cheese, Cracked Pepper, and Honey Drizzle

makes 8 small plates or 10 to 12 hors d'oeuvres

INGREDIENTS

8 ounces goat cheese (creamy chèvre, usually in a small log)

2–3 teaspoons chopped fresh basil or your herb of choice (tarragon is great, or you can substitute a prepared pesto, or use half the amount listed of dried herbs)

salt

24 ripe cherry tomatoes (preferably the larger ones)

½ cup honey

2 tablespoons peppercorns

PREPARATION

The filling can be made 2 to 3 days ahead of time, and will actually be more flavorful after chilling for more than a day.

Place the goat cheese in a mixing bowl and let it warm to room temperature for 15 minutes. During this time, finely chop the herbs and add them to the mixing bowl along with the salt. Begin to mix the cheese and herbs using a whisk, blending the cheese mixture until it's even and creamy. The mix can be stored, refrigerated and covered, for 2 to 3 days. It's easier to pipe the mixture if it has been chilled.

Wash and stem the tomatoes, and, using a paring knife, carefully slice a very thin piece off the bottom of each tomato to keep it from rolling around. Then, using the tip of the knife, carefully core the tomato by removing the pulp and seeds. The tomatoes can be stored for several hours.

To serve, place the cheese mixture in a pastry bag with a star tip and fill each tomato. Place three tomatoes on each plate, drizzle with honey, and sprinkle the plate with cracked pepper or liberally dust with freshly ground pepper from a pepper mill. Reserve some of the fresh herbs and sprinkle them on and around the plate for an extra hit of color and complementary flavor.

VARIATIONS

Fill the tomatoes with mozzarella, blue cheese, Cheddar, or cream cheese. You can also broil the tomatoes just before serving to lightly "gratin" the cheese; serve slightly warm.

Vegetable Spoon Explosions

Makes enough for 24 to 36 spoons

INGREDIENTS

¼ cup minced red bell pepper

¼ cup minced yellow bell pepper

¼ cup minced carrot

1 tablespoon minced garlic

2 tablespoons minced red onion

2 tablespoons minced fresh basil or cilantro

1 teaspoon salt

1 teaspoon freshly ground black pepper

6 ounces cream cheese

6 ounces creamy goat cheese

PREPARATION

Be sure to mince the vegetables very finely (no larger than half a match head) so that they'll flow easily through the tip of a pastry bag; you'll get an even distribution of all the vegetables in one little bite. Combine all ingredients except the cheeses in a bowl. Toss well and let sit while you prepare the cheeses.

Add the cheeses to a mixing bowl of a food processor or electric mixer and, using the paddle attachment and slow speed, mix until the cheeses are lightly blended (approximately 1 minute). Increase the speed to medium and blend for 2 minutes. Stop and scrape the bowl, and then add the vegetable mixture. Continue to blend the mixture on medium speed until the vegetables are just blended. Do not overmix, as the colors from the peppers will bleed out. Remove the mixture and refrigerate, covered, for an hour to firm the mix. You can prepare this 2 to 3 days in advance and keep in the refrigerator, but remove it an hour before using, to soften.

When you're ready to serve, fill a pastry bag using a large open star tip. Gather as many teaspoons as you need and simply pipe the cheese mixture into each spoon, filling with enough for a sufficient "explosion." Either pass the spoons around on a platter or set one spoon at each place setting using a small plate as an underliner.

You can customize the flavor of the cheese mixture by adding a number of different herbs or spices. I also enjoy making these with a southwestern flair by adding some jalapeños and chili powder for an extra-explosive hit!

Crab and Caviar Bomblets

Makes 4 servings

INGREDIENTS

½ cup sour cream

¼ cup mayonnaise

2 tablespoons minced red onion

1 tablespoon Dijon mustard

1 teaspoon salt

½ teaspoon ground black pepper

2 tablespoons cider vinegar

1 pound lump crabmeat

1 ounce caviar (your choice, based on your budget)

PREPARATION

Begin by combining all ingredients except the crab and caviar in a mixing bowl. Using a whisk, blend thoroughly until smooth. Add the crabmeat and mix with a spoon until well blended; do not overmix. Refrigerate for 30 minutes to let the mixture set up.

Using a standard-sized muffin tin, line the inside of each muffin cup with a piece of plastic wrap. There should be about 1 inch of extra wrap overhanging the sides.

Now place approximately 3 heaping tablespoons of the crab mixture into the bottom of each cup. Using the back of the spoon, press the crab mix firmly into the bottoms of the tin, lightly "feathering" the crab up the sides. The idea is to make a well in each cup.

Once the crab is portioned, place approximately 1 teaspoon of the caviar into the center of each crab pocket. Lightly press the caviar into the pocket and then place 2 more tablespoons of the crab mixture on top. Lightly press the crab mixture so that it's level with the flat surface of the tin.

Fold the extra film wrap over the crab bombs and refrigerate for at least 1 hour.

When you're ready to serve, remove the tin from the refrigerator and carefully remove each bomb from its cup by pulling the excess film wrap. Each bomb should still hold the shape of the cup. Place it upside down on a plate and carefully peel off the film wrap.

The bombs should be presented simply; they don't require any sauce. You can garnish the plate with a simple leaf of lettuce or 3 leaves of arugula. Serve with a wedge of lemon to be squeezed over the bombs for a little hint of citrus.

VARIATIONS

To make less costly bombs, you can use salmon caviar with great results.

Oven-Roasted Balsamic Olives

Makes 8 to 10 servings

INGREDIENTS

1 tablespoon olive oil

½ red onion

1 red bell pepper

6 garlic cloves

1 pound mixed olives
   (Calamata, Niçoise, Cerignilia, oil cured)

6 tablespoons balsamic vinegar

½ teaspoon cracked black pepper

2 sprigs fresh rosemary

PREPARATION

Preheat oven to 350 degrees.

Slice the onion into ½-inch-wide strips. Slice and deseed the red pepper and slice it into ½-by-1-inch strips. Peel the garlic cloves and lightly smash them.

Heat a 10-inch ovenproof sauté pan or cast-iron skillet over a medium flame. Add olive oil to coat the pan. Add the onion and pepper strips and sauté for 2 minutes Add the garlic cloves and sauté for 30 seconds, Add the olives and sauté while mixing for 2 minutes. Add the balsamic vinegar and mix well. Add the black pepper and rosemary sprigs, mix well, and bake for 12 to 15 minutes.

Remove from the oven and transfer to a serving bowl; you can also serve directly from a cast-iron pan, but be sure to use a trivet under it. The olives are eaten right out of the pan or bowl; be sure to have a small dish in which your guests can place the pits.

You can use any combination of olives, or even just one type if that's all you can find. This is one of my favorite ways to eat olives; the roasting brings out great fruity flavors, and the balsamic vinegar adds just enough acidity and helps provide some caramelization. It's super easy and the ultimate rustic presentation of olives. If you have any left over, they're great to use in salads or sauces. Just be sure to remove the pits!

Savory Palmiers with English Mustard

Makes approximately 24 palmiers

INGREDIENTS

1 puff pastry sheet

6 tablespoons coarse-grained mustard, such as Pommery

PREPARATION

Preheat oven to 400 degrees.

We use a commercial frozen puff pastry sheet at the Mist Grill, and you may want to as well. Making puff pastry from scratch is great but very time consuming and requires a level of skill that can be elusive for many chefs even after years of practice. There are several brands available in supermarkets; the Pepperidge Farms sheets are found almost everywhere, and their size and quality are perfect for most uses.

Remove the frozen sheet from the freezer and let it thaw for 20 to 30 minutes while still in the wrapper. If you try to work with the sheet while it's frozen, it'll crack.

Place the sheet on a lightly floured surface with the shortest side closest to you. Evenly coat the entire pastry sheet with the mustard. Starting at the bottom, begin to roll the sheet inward; evenly roll just to the center. Turn the sheet 180 degrees and roll the other side toward the middle, thus creating two pinwheels facing each other. The finished rolled sheet should be two equal circles joined at the center. Lightly press the roll to tighten it up and slightly flatten it. Wrap it tightly in plastic film wrap and freeze for at least 3 hours. This will keep in the freezer for approximately one month if kept wrapped tightly.

To serve, remove the roll from the freezer and let it thaw for 20 minutes. Slice the roll into ¼-inch slices and lay the pinwheels on a baking sheet that has been either lightly oiled or lined with parchment paper. Space the pinwheels about ½ inch apart. Bake for 10 to 12 minutes until golden brown. Serve immediately.

Tomato-Poached Shrimp

Makes 4 starter plates or 10 to 12 hors d'oeuvres

INGREDIENTS

1 pound shrimp (21–25 count per pound)

2 tablespoons vegetable oil

¼ cup minced red onion

¼ cup minced red bell pepper

1 tablespoon minced fresh garlic

2 cups tomato juice

6 tablespoons balsamic vinegar

2 tablespoons minced jalapeño peppers

3 tablespoons finely chopped fresh cilantro

2 tablespoons fresh lime juice

1 teaspoon salt

PREPARATION

Peel and devein the shrimp, leaving the tail segment on. Keep refrigerated until you're ready to cook.

In a medium saucepan, add the oil and heat until it's hot enough to sauté. Add the onion, red pepper, and garlic and sauté over high heat for 2 minutes or until the onions start to become transparent. Add the tomato juice and reduce the heat to a simmer. Add the balsamic vinegar and jalapeños and continue to simmer for 5 minutes. Add the cilantro, lime juice, and salt.

Add the shrimp to the tomato mixture and blend until the shrimp are completely covered by the sauce. Continue to simmer for approximately 3 minutes, until the shrimp are slightly firm and their flesh is white. Remove the pot from the heat and let it rest for 5 minutes.

Remove the shrimp from the tomato mixture and place them in a bowl. Cover lightly to allow heat to escape, and place in the refrigerator until fully chilled.

Remove the tomato mixture from the pot and place in a food processor fitted with an S blade. Completely puree the sauce and transfer to a clean bowl. Cover with plastic wrap and refrigerate until well chilled.

Arrange 4 to 6 shrimp on each plate and spoon 2 tablespoons of the sauce evenly over the shrimp. For a party, arrange the shrimp evenly around a platter. Fill a small bowl with sauce and place it in the center for dipping.

Mini Grilled Polenta Sandwich

Makes 12 mini sandwiches

PREPARATION

To make the polenta

In a heavy-bottomed saucepan, bring the milk and water to a boil. Reduce the heat to low and begin to add the cornmeal while stirring with a wooden spoon. Add the cornmeal in a very slow, steady stream to avoid clumping. Continue to stir vigorously; this mini aerobics course will continue for about 15 to 20 minutes. The polenta is done when it appears smooth and slightly creamy and pulls easily from the sides of the pot. Add the salt, pepper, and the grated Parmesan and blend until the cheese is fully incorporated.

Pour the polenta into a pregreased 9-by-4-inch bread pan, making sure to scrape out every bit. Using the back of a wooden spoon, push the polenta fully into the pan and smooth the top into a level surface. Cover with plastic wrap and refrigerate for at least 3 hours. This can be also prepped a day ahead.

To make the sandwiches

Preheat oven to 350 degrees.

Begin by removing the polenta loaf from the pan. First, run a knife around the sides of the pan to loosen the polenta, then flip the loaf onto a cutting board; it should slide out. If it doesn't at first, try it again, this time slamming it a bit harder!

Once the polenta is on the cutting board, slice the loaf down the middle from end to end, creating two equal loaves. Then slice

INGREDIENTS

- 1 cup whole milk
- 2 cups water
- 1 cup coarse cornmeal
- 1 teaspoon salt
- ¼ cup grated Parmesan cheese
- ¼ cup olive oil
- 3 ripe plum tomatoes
- 8 ounces mozzarella
- 12 fresh spinach leaves
- 1 teaspoon ground black pepper

across the loaf in ½-inch slices. Do this to both loaves; you should have approximately 24 polenta squares.

In a large skillet, heat the olive oil until very hot. You can test it by placing a small piece of polenta in the oil. It should snap, crackle, pop, and brown almost immediately. If the oil isn't hot enough, it'll soak into the polenta, which won't brown properly.

Once the oil is ready, quickly brown all the squares on both sides, then use a spatula to transfer them to a clean baking sheet or onto parchment paper. Let the squares cool.

Slice the tomatoes into ¼-inch slices. Place 1 slice on each of 12 squares. Slice the mozzarella into ⅛-inch-thick squares to equal the dimensions of the polenta squares. Place the cheese on the tomatoes, then place a spinach leaf on the

continued next page

21

cheese. Place the other 12 squares onto the bases and put all the sandwiches on a baking sheet. Bake for 6 to 8 minutes or until the cheese just begins to melt out of the middle.

Pass on a platter, as hors d'oeuvres, or put each sandwich onto a small plate. You can use some of the extra spinach leaves as garnish.

VARIATIONS

I sometimes use a basil or arugula leaf in place of the spinach. You can also replace the tomatoes with a slice of roasted red or yellow pepper. And try substituting creamy goat cheese for your more adventurous crowds!

LEAFY THINGS

Maybe we here in Vermont are so passionate about our salads because our long winters and brief, intense summers bring us such a limited season of greens from the garden. We at the Mist Grill are blessed to be able to get great organic greens from a fine network of local farmers. The arrival of these goodies causes a lot of nervous anticipation in our kitchen. Whether it's succulent bibb lettuce, tangy and smoky arugula, red-leaf romaine, bitter dandelion greens, ruddy wilted beet tops, curly frisé, or sharp mizuna, all make their way from Vermont's fields to our salad station.

Many of us grew up in the days when salad meant chopped-up iceberg lettuce in a bowl, with perhaps some quartered tomatoes and carrot shavings. In many ways salad was often only a surface on which to pour some form of gloppy bottled dressing.

My epiphany came when I was twelve and sat down for a special dinner at one of America's best-known steakhouses, Peter Luger's in Brooklyn. The old waiter served me a bowl of iceberg lettuce topped with slices of red onion, ripe tomatoes, and blue cheese. It's still one of my favorite combinations, and I've included my recipe with a slightly updated Balsamic Vinaigrette dressing.

In most parts of the world, though, iceberg was an anomaly. The Italians, I'm sure, have been munching on arugula and radicchio for centuries, but most contemporary Americans didn't "discover" alternatives to iceberg until the very early 1980s, when salads started becoming a more important part of diets, and the salad course came to represent a place for fresh innovation.

In many ways the salad course has become the ultimate canvas for culinary creativity. The subtle natural flavors of many greens—whether slightly bitter, grassy, sweet, or even smoky—allow for a multitude of options. Their crisp textures work well when paired with soft cheeses, bits of sliced fruit, or crunchy nuts.

The fresher the greens are, the better. Fortunately, most good markets now understand the demand for unique greens and are doing a good job of handling them. As a shopper, you should feel free to ask questions about any product and how to prepare it. But it's your responsibility to inspect the greens for freshness. They should all have good, vibrant color, be clean, and not show the slightest bit of wilt. If in doubt, pick off a small piece to taste to get an idea of its flavor, especially if the green is new to you. There's now a good year-round supply of interesting greens from warm climates, so keep your eyes peeled in winter as well as summer.

At the Mist Grill we never limit ourselves to just greens when we compose a salad. We also use other seasonal vegetables to create salads that can also serve as side dishes during the summer months—maybe grilled fresh corn kernels tossed with julienned roasted red peppers and slivered red onion, or paper-thin shaved fennel with blood oranges and prosciutto. Both are outstanding complements to a plate of ribs or barbecued chicken. We also craft salads in the dark and cold Vermont winters that serve as great palate cleansers and fulfilling appetizers. Vermonters are known for putting up foods and making do during the long winters, so we, too, take that rustic approach, incorporating creamy local goat cheeses, caramelized apples and pears, or finely shaved beets into our salads. During the winter months our salads might also feature hearty greens such as winter spinach and blends of mesclun. In many cases we'll shave thin slices of parsnips and other root vegetables and then deep-fry them to create a wonderful, crunchy nest of golden wisps to lie atop the greens.

We'll also tenderize hearty greens such as Swiss chard, heating them for warm salads. These are wonderful foundations for the addition of fruits and of vinaigrettes that use reduced fruit juices as a component. Several of the recipes in this book include fruit in the dressings. Citrus in particular makes a great addition to dressings, not only for imparting flavor but also by providing acidity without the harshness of vinegar.

As you begin to explore our leafy things recipes, you'll find that you can customize them to your liking or to use whatever ingredients you have on hand. Making excellent salads, in fact, doesn't require strict guidelines; just learn the basics and you're on your own. Hit the garden or the farm stand soon, experiment by using these recipes as starting points, and start to enjoy the freshness of nature's unadulterated goodies!

Mist Greens with Robin's Sherry Vinaigrette

Makes 4 to 6 salads

INGREDIENTS

⅓ cup sherry vinegar

3 tablespoons Dijon mustard

1 cup olive oil

1 teaspoon salt

½ teaspoon ground black pepper

4 cups mesclun salad mix (or greens of your choice)

PREPARATION

In a food processor fitted with an S blade, add the sherry vinegar and Dijon mustard. Process for 15 seconds. While the machine is on, slowly drizzle in the oil until it's fully incorporated; this should be done over the course of about 45 seconds. Add the salt and pepper and remove the dressing to a clean container. The dressing should be emulsified and slightly creamy. It will hold in a refrigerator for up to a week but may require shaking to re-emulsify if it has become separated.

When you're ready to serve the salad, place the (washed and dried) greens in a large salad bowl. Add approximately ½ cup of the dressing uniformly around the greens. Use a pair of tongs to toss the salad to evenly coat with the dressing. Serve immediately from the bowl or place equal amounts onto plates.

The simplicity of this dressing is wonderful, and the sherry vinegar gives it a tangy punch that our diners crave!

Shaved Fennel and Parmesan with Prosciutto and Blood Orange Vinaigrette

Makes 4 salads

INGREDIENTS

1 large fresh fennel bulb

½ cup fresh-squeezed blood orange juice (you can substitute regular orange juice)

1½ tablespoons Dijon mustard

1½ tablespoons minced fresh shallots

½ tablespoon minced fresh tarragon *or* ½ teaspoon dried

1 teaspoon salt

¼ teaspoon ground white pepper

1 6-ounce wedge fresh Parmesan cheese

8 paper-thin slices prosciutto (approximately ½ pound)

PREPARATION

To prepare the fennel

Trim off the fennel tops and cut the bulb in half from top to bottom. Trim out the core and begin to slice very slowly and with a very sharp knife. The key to success is absolutely paper-thin slices of fennel—so thin you can almost see through them!

Once the fennel is sliced, store it in a container with a damp paper towel on top. Cover with plastic wrap and set aside until you're ready to use it. I suggest not holding it for more than 2 hours, or the fennel will start to brown.

To make the vinaigrette

Use a food processor fitted with an S blade. Add the orange juice and Dijon mustard, and process for 15 to 20 seconds. With the machine still running, slowly drizzle in the oil; this should take about 45 seconds. Stop the machine and add the minced shallots, tarragon, salt, and pepper. Pulse the machine three times for 2 seconds each.

Transfer the dressing to a container. This dressing is not meant to be a thick emulsion; it will be light in body. You may need to stir well before serving.

To shave the Parmesan

Make sure the cheese is well chilled. Using a sharp vegetable peeler, slowly "peel" or shave ribbons of cheese from the wedge. You want to have at least 4 ribbons approximately 3 inches long and ¾-inch wide per salad.

To assemble the salad

Place one-quarter of the shaved fennel on the center of each plate. Try to bundle it up so it's as compact and high as possible. Lay 2 slices of prosciutto on each plate, around the fennel mound, with the prosciutto slightly wrapping or "caressing" the fennel. Place a ribbon of shaved cheese across the top of the fennel. Drizzle with 2 to 3 tablespoons of dressing. Serve immediately.

Warm Spinach with Pan-Roasted Pears, Stilton, and Cranberry Vinaigrette

Makes 4 large salads

INGREDIENTS

1 pound spinach

2 pears

2 tablespoons butter

3 tablespoons sugar

½ cup dried cranberries

½ cup cranberry juice

2 tablespoons minced shallots

1 cup canola or grapeseed oil

1 teaspoon salt

½ teaspoon ground black pepper

8 ounces Stilton cheese

PREPARATION

Preheat oven to 350 degrees.

Wash and destem the spinach and dry it well. Cover and refrigerate until you're ready to assemble the salads.

Peel the pears and cut them into 8 equal wedges. In a sauté pan over medium heat, melt the butter, add the sugar, and stir. Add the pears to the pan and toss until they're completely coated with the sugar mix. Continue to cook over medium heat while turning the pears. The pears should be evenly browned and caramelized; depending on how ripe they are, this may take from 8 to 12 minutes. The pears should be fork-tender when done. Remove the pears and put them on a plate until you're ready to use them.

Add the dried cranberries to the pan and lightly sauté for 2 minutes. Immediately pour the cranberry juice into the sauté pan to deglaze the butter and sugar: Using a spatula or wooden spoon, gently scrape the butter and sugar into the juice and stir to incorporate. Do not let the juice simmer; quickly pour the mix into a stainless-steel mixing bowl.

Add the shallots, oil, salt, and pepper. Vigorously whisk the dressing until it's fully blended and slightly emulsified.

Crumble the Stilton into thumbnail-sized pieces and store in a bowl.

To assemble the salad, place equal amounts of spinach on each plate.

Place the pears on a baking sheet and bake for 8 minutes.

In a saucepan, add the dressing and begin to heat over a low flame, whisking occasionally. The dressing should be warm, but do not let it come to a simmer.

Place the pears on top of the spinach, 2 wedges per plate. Sprinkle equal amounts of the Stilton around each salad. Ladle 3 tablespoons of the warm dressing over the salad and serve immediately.

Bibb Lettuce with Roasted Red Pepper Dressing, Toasted Pistachios, and Goat Cheese

Makes 4 large salads

½ cup roasted red pepper puree or three whole fresh red peppers

4 garlic cloves

1 tablespoon finely chopped fresh rosemary

1 teaspoon salt

½ teaspoon ground black pepper

2 tablespoons Dijon mustard

⅓ cup white wine vinegar

1 cup olive oil

½ cup shelled uncolored pistachios

8 ounces creamy goat cheese (chèvre log)

2–3 heads bibb lettuce

PREPARATION

I suggest purchasing prepared roasted peppers; there are several very good producers, and you can find them either canned or bottled in most good stores. Still, roasting your own is fairly easy, and the salad will be a little tastier due to the freshness of the peppers.

To roast the peppers

Preheat your charcoal grill; if you have a gas stove, they can be roasted over an open flame right on your rangetop. First, wash and dry the peppers, then lightly coat them with a little olive oil, using your hand. They should be coated enough just to be glistening, but not dripping.

Using a pair of tongs, place the peppers on the grill or open flame. Rotate the peppers until they're fully charred and black all over. Place the peppers in a bowl and cover tightly with plastic wrap. Let the peppers cool for 30 minutes. Remove all the charred skin—which has now become loosened from the meat of the pepper—by gently using your fingers to peel it off. When the peppers are cleaned, split them down the middle and remove all the seed and stem centers. These fillets can be used for numerous dishes!

To make the dressing

Place the pepper fillets in a food processor fitted with an S blade. Run the machine to rough-chop the peppers. Stop the machine and add the garlic, rosemary, salt, pepper, Dijon mustard, and vinegar. Process again for approximately 60 seconds, or until the ingredients appear to be smooth and pureed. With the machine still running, add the oil very slowly until it's fully incorporated. Transfer the dressing to a clean container and set aside or refrigerate until needed.

To toast the pistachios

Add a drizzle of olive oil to a sauté pan to coat the surface and place it over low heat. Add the pistachios and toss continuously for 3 to 5 minutes, until the nuts just begin to smell roasted or "nutty" and begin to brown. Remove immediately, as they will continue to cook even off the flame. Transfer to a dish and set aside.

To assemble the salad

Carefully peel the bibb lettuce leaves from the head, keeping the lettuce "cups" intact. Arrange 5 to 6 cups loosely on each plate, starting from the center of the plate and moving out. Slice the goat cheese log into 8 medallions and place 2 medallions on the center of each plate atop the lettuce. Sprinkle the toasted pistachios in and around the lettuce cups. Ladle 3 tablespoons of dressing over each salad.

The Steak House Wedge

Makes 4 large salads

INGREDIENTS

1 red onion

2 ripe beefsteak tomatoes (you can substitute others as long as they're ripe)

8 ounces blue cheese (Gorgonzola is recommended)

1 head iceberg lettuce

1 cup Balsamic Vinaigrette (see page 151)

PREPARATION

Peel, then slice the onion into paper-thin rings and separate. Wash and slice the tomatoes into wedges—approximately 6 wedges per tomato. Crumble the blue cheese into thumbnail-sized pieces. Peel the outer leaves of the iceberg lettuce and remove the core. Slice the lettuce head into 4 equal wedges (6 if it's a very large head). Place each wedge on a plate. Put 4 tomato wedges on each plate surrounding the lettuce, then put 6 to 8 red onion rings across, apply a liberal dose of blue cheese, and drizzle the balsamic dressing over the whole plate. Enjoy!

Summer Tomatoes with Arugula, Steve's Spiced Pecans, and Balsamic Vinaigrette

Makes 4 servings

INGREDIENTS

2 tablespoons butter

1 cup pecan halves

2 tablespoons sugar

1 teaspoon salt

1 teaspoon ground black pepper

3 tablespoons balsamic vinegar

2 bunches arugula

4 juice ripe tomatoes

1 cup Balsamic Vinaigrette (see page 151)

PREPARATION

To prepare the pecans

Melt the butter in a 10-inch sauté pan over medium heat. Add the pecans and begin to toss with the butter. As soon as you detect the slightest browning on the pecans, sprinkle the sugar evenly over them while tossing. Add the salt and pepper and mix evenly. Watch as the sugar begins to melt and caramelize onto the nuts. As soon as the sugar is melted and adhering to the nuts, add the balsamic vinegar and quickly toss well to evenly coat the nuts and deglaze the pan. Remove the nuts to a large plate and spread them out into a single layer. The nuts will be very hot; do not use your fingers! They'll cool within 10 minutes. These tasty morsels make a great snack all by themselves and can be used as topping for numerous recipes.

To assemble the salad

Destem and wash the arugula very well. You may want to wash twice to ensure that there's no sand or grit. There's nothing worse than crunching down on something in your salad that shouldn't be there!

Arrange the arugula in a circle on the plate, with the stem portion in the center. Slice the tomatoes into ¼-inch-thick slices and stack 4 or 5 on top of each other in the center of the arugula. Place 6 to 8 pecans around the rim of the plate and drizzle 3 tablespoons of the Balsamic Vinaigrette over the tomatoes and arugula. Serve immediately.

SMALL PLATES

Vermont must have more antiques stores per capita then any other state, and this provides us at the Mist Grill with a never-ending treasure trove of old plates and silverware. We love spending hours digging through piles of mismatched stuff that no one else really wants. An afternoon driving around the countryside discovering a new antiques shop or flea market makes for great entertainment as well as giving us a chance to restock our shelves with cool, funky old stuff.

Adding to the rustic patina of the restaurant, old plates from old farmhouses help instill a certain sense of history and nostalgia. When our guests are presented an attractive dish on a plate that they might recognize as one that Grandmother used to have, it adds to the dining experience, I think.

Not only does the use of nonmatching plates provide an ever changing presentation style from dish to dish, but from a practical side, we never have to worry about replacing matched china. And with most of the plates costing about 50 cents, we don't care, either!

People comment all the time about the mismatched stuff we use, and seem to unanimously approve of our "recycling efforts." We even go as far as using slate roofing tiles from old buildings as platters for various combinations, including our famous ploughman's lunch. Don't feel restricted to using your standard dishes and plates when planning a dinner or luncheon. Many times the use of wacky alternatives can provide not only a different look at the table, but also instant conversational fuel for the guests.

Whether you elect to use your finest Limoges or an eclectic mix of china, inevitably the food that ends up on them is what really counts. Our "small plates" at the Mist Grill represent the section of the menu where we try to make a great first impression. It's important to present a good mix to entice our guests to explore flavors or ingredients that they may not have tried or aren't sure they want for a main course.

With small plates, I spend a little more time on a complex presentation of the dish, because this course sets the stage for the rest of the meal. I still take a simple approach to the preparation of the ingredients, but it takes more thought to highlight the ingredients and present multiple dimensions of flavor in a miniature version of a dish. Think of the saying, "Ten pounds of flavor in a five-pound bag." For me, it's important to make sure that every bite holds several elements of the dish and delivers bold flavor and different textures. Even in a recipe as simple sounding as Smoked Trout Cakes with Horseradish Crème Fraîche, every bite holds great flavor as part of a multifaceted dish.

Our small plates are not considered fancy or high-tech sorts of appetizers, but we focus a little more on using simple garnishes to highlight the plate and add that little extra touch of color or texture to make a statement. You'll find the recipes are simple yet interesting, while allowing for some extra touches to create a memorable dish.

With these dishes, something the French call *mise en place* is very important. Simply put, *mise en place* means preassembling all the ingredients in proper condition—chopped, peeled, measured, and so forth—for preparation. Believe me, having everything in order so you need only plate the food makes it a lot easier to entertain guests who are waiting at the table. It also gives you an extra last minute to apply the cool garnish or drizzle of sauce that gives the dish a special look. This philosophy applies everywhere, but especially to the small plates. The first dish you offer your guests should come out on time; it should say that you're confident in the food you're serving, and you'll be able to actually join the party!

Our small plates recipes meet these criteria, and all have some flexibility in the use of ingredients. Introduce your own special interpretations once you've realized how easy they are to prepare. I think you'll find that the recipes deliver great country-style appetizers that are neither difficult nor complex, but add a bit of excitement when they're served.

Warm Stilton Flan with Grilled Pears and Brown Bread

Makes 6 to 8 flans

INGREDIENTS

2 whole eggs

3 egg yolks

2 cups half-and-half

2 teaspoons salt

1 teaspoon ground black pepper

6 ounces crumbled Stilton

6 slices pumpernickel bread

3 pears

3 tablespoons sugar

3 tablespoons balsamic vinegar

PREPARATION

Preheat the oven to 350 degrees. Preheat the charcoal grill to medium.

In a mixing bowl, add the eggs and egg yolks and whisk until blended and smooth. Add the half-and-half, salt, pepper, and Stilton. Whisk until the mixture is well blended but the crumbled cheese isn't too broken up.

Take six empty ovenproof ramekins (4- to 6-ounce capacity), place one upside down on top of a slice of the pumpernickel bread and, with a small knife, cut around the rim of the ramekin to create a bread disk that's the size of the top circumference. Repeat with all 6 slices; keep the bread disks uncovered so they begin to dry out.

Rub the inside of six ramekins with butter to evenly coat each. Using a ladle, portion the flan mix into each ramekin; be sure to stir the mix each time to ensure that you have a good dispersion of the cheese. Otherwise the cheese will settle to the bottom of the mixing bowl.

Place the ramekins in a small roasting pan.

Fill the pan with enough *hot* tap water to come halfway up the sides of the ramekins. Carefully place the roasting pan in the oven, being careful not to slosh the water too much and give the flans a bath that they don't want to take. Bake the flans for 20 minutes; their tops should be slightly congealed and barely firm to the touch.

While the flans are baking, peel the pears and cut them into 6 halves, from top to bottom. In a mixing bowl, toss the pears with the sugar and vinegar and let them sit for 10 minutes to soak up some of the liquid.

Place the pears on the preheated grill (if you don't have a grill, place the pears in a small roasting pan and roast for 20 minutes). Using a pair of tongs, grill the pears for approximately 3 to 5 minutes on each side, or until the sides are browned and the pears are beginning to soften. Remove the pears and keep them warm.

After the flans have baked for 20 minutes,

continued next page

carefully place a bread disk on top of each flan and gently press the disk onto the flan. The disks should be just sitting on the surface.

Bake for 10 to 15 minutes longer, then remove the flans from the oven and let them sit in the water bath for 10 minutes. This will ensure that they are fully set, and that the water bath has cooled enough to remove the flans safely. Run the tip of a small knife blade around the sides of each ramekin to loosen the flans.

To assemble the dish

Turn the flans out onto a plate and tap their bottoms to help them slide out of the ramekins. Take each pear and, from top to bottom, starting just below the stem area, slice through it, once down the center and then once to the right and left of center, creating a fan effect. Place each pear with the stem side just resting on the edge of the top of each flan. Garnish the plate by placing a sprig of fresh parsley on top of the flan. Serve immediately.

Smoked Trout Cakes with Horseradish Crème Fraîche

Makes about 24 cakes (12 servings)

INGREDIENTS

½ cup celery, ⅛-inch dice

½ cup onions, ⅛-inch dice

½ cup apples, ⅛-inch dice
(any type; you can leave the skin on)

3 tablespoons canola or olive oil

2 pounds smoked trout fillets
(approximately 6 fillets)

¼ cup capers

1 cup mayonnaise

3 egg yolks

¼ cup Dijon mustard

2 tablespoons salt

1 teaspoon ground black pepper

¼ cup lemon juice

3 cups fresh bread crumbs

2 cups crème fraîche *or* sour cream

¼ cup prepared horseradish

2 tablespoons Worcestershire sauce

Canola oil for frying

PREPARATION

In a large sauté pan, add the oil, celery, onions, and apples. Sauté over high heat while stirring for 6 to 8 minutes or until the onions are translucent and have begun to caramelize. Remove the vegetables to a large mixing bowl and let them cool.

Remove the skin from the trout and crumble all the meat into the vegetable mixture. The trout should be in ¼-inch chunks. Add the capers.

In another, smaller mixing bowl, add the mayonnaise, egg yolks, Dijon mustard, salt, and pepper. Whisk well until creamy and smooth. Add the lemon juice and whisk again to fully incorporate.

Add the bread crumbs to the vegetable mixture and begin to mix all the ingredients well. Add the mayonnaise mixture and, using your hands, blend until the mix is uniform.

Using a 2-ounce ice-cream scoop, scoop out balls of the mixture and place them on a cookie sheet. Continue until you've emptied the mixing bowl. Use your fingers to form the balls into mini cake shapes by pressing down on them and then forming the sides. You can also do this in your hand to better compact the mixture. Refrigerate for at least 1 hour before cooking.

To make the Horseradish Crème Fraîche

In a small mixing bowl, whisk together the crème fraîche, horseradish, and Worcestershire until fully blended. Refrigerate until you're ready to use it.

continued next page

To assemble the plates

In a heavy-bottomed sauté pan, add enough canola oil to fill the pan about ⅛ inch deep. Heat the oil to just below the smoke point or approximately 350 degrees. Using a spatula, carefully place the trout cakes in the oil and fry for about 2 minutes per side or until they're golden brown and begin to crisp on the edges. Remove from the pan. Place two cakes in the center of each plate. Put a dollop of the crème fraîche mixture on each side of the cakes; you can garnish with a slice of lemon and some chopped lettuce or herbs if you desire. The simplicity of the cakes is wonderful—they look great without much adornment.

Grilled Shrimp on Creamy Grits with Tomato Chili Puree

Makes 4 servings

INGREDIENTS

16 shrimp (10–12 count per pound)

3 tablespoons olive oil, divided

1½ teaspoons salt, divided

½ teaspoon black pepper

½ cup diced onions

½ cup diced green chili pepper (poblano or Anaheim)

4 garlic cloves

8 plum tomatoes

½ cup water

2 tablespoons chopped fresh cilantro

1½ cups milk

½ cup quick grits

½ cup shredded Cheddar cheese

2 tablespoons butter

1 tablespoon fresh thyme

PREPARATION

To prepare the shrimp

Peel and devein the shrimp and toss them with 2 tablespoons of olive oil, 1 teaspoon of the salt, and the black pepper. Keep this mixture chilled until you're ready to cook.

To make the sauce

Dice the onions, peppers, and garlic. Chop the tomatoes into ½-inch pieces. In a medium saucepan over high heat, add enough olive oil (1 tablespoon) to coat the bottom of the pan. Add the diced onions and cook while stirring for 4 minutes, or until they begin to caramelize and are translucent. Add the diced peppers and sauté for 4 minutes longer. Add the garlic and cook for 1 minute, then add the tomatoes and sauté for 3 minutes. Reduce the heat to a simmer, add the water, and continue to cook for 4 minutes longer.

Remove the pan from the heat and let it cool. Place the sauce mix in a food processor fitted with an S blade and puree completely until smooth. Add the remaining salt and adjust the seasoning if desired. Transfer to a clean container and add the chopped cilantro. Mix well and set aside until you're ready to use.

To prepare the grits

In a heavy-bottomed saucepan, bring the milk to a simmer. Slowly add the grits while stirring until they're fully incorporated. (Follow the directions on the box, as the cooking time and amount of milk may vary.) The quick grits generally only cook for approximately 5 minutes. When the grits are creamy and fully cooked, add the shredded Cheddar and blend well. Add salt to taste, then add the butter and blend well. The grits should be eaten

continued next page

immediately, so they're best prepared just before serving.

To assemble the dish

Preheat the charcoal grill to high. In a saucepan, bring the tomato sauce to a simmer. When the grits are ready, place the shrimp on the grill and cook for 1½ to 2 minutes per side. Shrimp cook very quickly; when they're pink and just barely firm to the touch, remove them immediately.

Place a large spoonful (about 3 heaping tablespoons) of the grits on the center of each plate, then place 4 shrimp to circle each mound of grits. Ladle approximately 6 tablespoons of the tomato sauce around the shrimp and grits. You can garnish with a sprinkle or a sprig of cilantro.

Cappelini alla Black Walnut

Makes 4 large or 6 small portions

An old favorite from my New York restaurant
that has a simple, fresh taste I could eat every day!

INGREDIENTS

1 pound cappellini (angel hair pasta)

2 tablespoons olive oil

4 large ripe tomatoes *or* 6–8 plum tomatoes

½ cup finely diced red onions

¼ cup minced fresh basil

1 cup Balsamic Vinaigrette (see page 151)

2 teaspoons salt

1 teaspoon black pepper

1 pound fresh mozzarella

¼ cup freshly grated Parmesan cheese

PREPARATION

In a large stockpot, bring 2 to 3 quarts of water to a boil and add the pasta. Cook until al dente, or approximately 5 minutes. The pasta will be served chilled, so be sure to test it for doneness before removing it from the pot. Strain the pasta and run cold water over it to chill quickly. Transfer to a clean container and lightly toss with the olive oil to coat.

Dice the tomatoes to a ¼-inch size and add to a bowl. Add the diced onions and basil and toss well. Add ½ cup Balsamic Vinaigrette, along with the salt and pepper. Toss the mix well and let sit at room temperature for at least 30 minutes. This mixture can be prepared the day before and kept refrigerated, but be sure to remove it from the fridge at least 30 minutes before serving. The flavors are more bold and luscious when at room temperature.

Slice the fresh mozzarella into ¼-inch-thick disks and set aside. Grate the Parmesan and set aside.

To assemble the dish

In a soup or pasta bowl, place approximately 1 cup of the pasta. Stir the tomato mixture well to ensure that all the ingredients are well coated with the vinaigrette. Spoon ¼ cup of the tomato mixture over the pasta. Place 3 slices of the mozzarella across the top of the pasta and tomatoes. Drizzle 2 tablespoons of the vinaigrette evenly around the bowl. Sprinkle some of the grated Parmesan over the top. Garnish with a leaf of the basil. Repeat for each serving.

Thai Peanut Butter and Jelly with Mesclun and Orange Soy Dressing

Makes 4 sandwiches

This dish may sound odd, but it's really a surprisingly exciting spin on the classic PB&J. Inspired during a working visit from Tim and Richard Smucker, I had to follow through on the idea and put it on the menu to try it out on some customers. The result was super and has made the grade for this book!

INGREDIENTS

Rolls

1 cup creamy peanut butter

2 tablespoons sesame oil

6 tablespoons low-sodium soy sauce

¼ cup minced scallions

¼ teaspoon cayenne pepper

1 cup Smuckers Apricot Preserves

3 tablespoons grated fresh gingerroot

2 tablespoons grated lemon rind

1 tablespoon seeded and minced serrano or jalapeño peppers

8 slices white bread (the Wonder kind)

Dressing and Salad

2 cups mesclun mix

8 oranges (enough to make 1 cup juice)

1½ tablespoons sesame oil

3 tablespoons low-sodium soy sauce

2 tablespoons diced scallions

1 tablespoon freshly grated gingerroot

¼ cup rice vinegar

2 tablespoons Dijon mustard

1 teaspoon sesame seeds

PREPARATION

To prepare the rolls

Place the peanut butter in a mixing bowl and add the sesame oil and soy sauce. Using a whisk, slowly blend until all the ingredients are fully mixed. Add the diced scallions and cayenne pepper; mix well. In another bowl, add the apricot preserves, grated ginger, lemon rind, and minced peppers.

Remove the crusts from the white bread using a sharp knife. Place a slice between two pieces of plastic wrap. With a rolling pin, roll the bread out until it's about one and a half times larger. Don't roll it too thin or it'll tear apart later in the process.

Once you have all the bread rolled out, place a slice on a piece of plastic wrap (the wrap will be used to help form the roll). Spread a thin layer of the peanut butter across the bread, covering the entire surface. Take another slice and spread a thin layer of the apricot across the entire surface. Place the apricot slice on top of the peanut butter slice, with the apricot side facing up. Carefully start to roll them up like a jelly roll or sushi roll. Use the plastic wrap to help compress the bread as you go. When you have rolled the slices together, use the plastic wrap to tightly cover the roll. Repeat the process for the 4 rolls and keep refrigerated for at least 1 hour.

To make the dressing

Squeeze the oranges to get 1 cup of juice, or use a good-quality orange juice. If you elect to use fresh oranges, I suggest grating enough rind to add 2 tablespoons to the dressing.

Add all the ingredients except the mesclun at once to a food processor or blender and process until completely blended and slightly foamy.

Remove and store the dressing in a clean container until you're ready to use it. If you hold it for more than a few minutes, be prepared to need to rewhisk the dressing before use.

To assemble the dish

Remove the rolls from the refrigerator and remove the plastic wrap from each one. Place ½ cup of the mesclun mix on the center of each plate. Drizzle or ladle approximately 3 tablespoons of the dressing onto the greens. With a sharp knife, slice a roll in half, then slice each half in half again, but cut them on a slight bias. Place the four pieces of the roll symmetrically around the plate surrounding the mesclun. Drizzle a few drops of the dressing around the edges of the plates and rolls. Serve immediately.

Purple Potato *Causa* Topped with Pulled Chicken and Balsamic Vinaigrette

Makes 8 servings

This dish is a super summertime appetizer, and can be easily prepared a day ahead. The recipe is a variation on Doug Rodriquez's Peruvian *causa* dish, and I've taken the liberty of doing several versions. Basically a *causa* is a potato salad, but with some different twists. Before you start this recipe, you'll need to go to the hardware store! To create the stacks that you see in many restaurant presentations, you need something to serve as a mold, and your best bet is the PVC pipe that you can find at a hardware store. All you need is about 2 feet of pipe, although they'll probably want to sell you a standard pipe—6 to 8 feet long. You also want pipe with a 2-inch inner dimension. At a good lumberyard or hardware store, they may cut it for you, but if not you'll need a hacksaw to cut it yourself.

To make the molds, simply measure the pipe into 3-inch lengths—as many as you like— and cut. The result is pipe segments 3 inches high by 2 inches wide. The edges will be rough, so use fine-grit sandpaper to smooth them well; then run the segments through a dishwasher to clean them well. These PVC molds are very useful for many different cold molded foods. Do not attempt to use them in any cooking applications.

INGREDIENTS

- 4 large bone-in chicken breasts
- 2 teaspoons cumin powder
- 2 teaspoons chili powder
- 1 teaspoon garlic salt
- 10 purple potatoes
- ½ cup olive oil
- ¼ cup white vinegar
- ¼ cup Dijon mustard
- 2 teaspoons salt
- 1 teaspoon ground pepper
- ½ cup pitted and diced Calamata olives
- 1 cup diced tomatoes
- 4 teaspoons minced capers
- 2 teaspoons minced garlic
- ½ cup Balsamic Vinaigrette (see page 151)

PREPARATION

To prepare the chicken

Preheat the oven to 350 degrees. Wash and dry the chicken. Combine the cumin, chili powder, and garlic salt in a small bowl, then sprinkle the mix evenly over the skin side of the chicken.

Roast the chicken for 18 to 20 minutes until the juices run clear and the skin is well crisped. Let the chicken rest and cool. It can be refrigerated until you're ready to use it in the next steps.

To prepare the potatoes

Cut the potatoes into ½- by ¾-inch cubes, place them in boiling water, and cook for approximately 15 minutes, until they're fork-tender. Drain the potatoes and put them in a mixing bowl. Add the olive oil, vinegar, Dijon mustard, salt, and pepper. Using a hand potato masher, mash the potatoes until they're well blended but still chunky. Let the mixture cool.

Combine the olives, tomatoes, capers, and garlic in a bowl.

To assemble the dish

Begin by rubbing the insides of the PVC mold with some olive oil—just enough to coat the surface. Place the molds on a tray or large plate, scoop 3 tablespoons of the potato mix into each mold, and press down firmly. Sprinkle 2 tablespoons of the tomato mixture into each mold and press down. Add more of the potato mixture to fill the rest of the mold and again, press down firmly. Place in the refrigerator for at least 1 hour so the stacks set up and can be unmolded easily.

Using your fingers, pull all the chicken meat and skin from the bones and continue to pull the meat apart so it looks evenly shredded. Be sure to use all the skin; you may want to use a knife to julienne it.

When you're ready to serve, remove the molds from the refrigerator and place one on each plate. Carefully push the filling down while you are pulling the mold upward and off. They should unmold easily. Place approximately 2 tablespoons of the pulled chicken on top of each stack and sprinkle some of the extra around the base of the molds. Sprinkle some of the remaining tomato mixture around the plate, then drizzle 3 tablespoons of the Balsamic Vinaigrette on the stacks and around the plates. Serve immediately.

Salmon and Tuna Sashimi Towers with Wasabi Cream and Sesame Oil

Makes 4 towers

This dish is simple to make and absolutely fabulous. The key is getting superfresh salmon and tuna from your fish supplier. Tell them that you're using it for a raw dish, and that they must make sure it's sushi quality!

Just when you thought those PVC molds (see Peruvian Potato *Causa* on page 48) were destined for the closet until you made the *causa* again, here's another use for them.

PREPARATION

On a clean and sanitized cutting board, and using a sharp knife, slice the tuna into ½-inch strips. Then dice the strips until the tuna is well chopped and begins to become slightly sticky. Place the minced tuna in a clean bowl and add 1 teaspoon of the salt and 2 teaspoons of the scallions. Blend well.

Clean the cutting board well and repeat the exact process for the salmon.

Be sure the PVC molds are well cleaned. Coat the inside surface with olive oil. Place the molds on the plates you'll be serving on and fill each one a third full with the salmon. Add 1 tablespoon of the diced tomatoes, then add tuna to fill the remainder of the mold. Try to use equal amounts of tuna and salmon per mold. Press dowm firmly on the mixture so it'll form and set up. Refrigerate for at least 1 hour.

To make the dressing

Put the wasabi powder in a mixing bowl and add the vinegar. Using a fork or small whisk,

INGREDIENTS

- 1 pound sushi-quality yellowfin or ahi tuna
- 2 teaspoons salt
- 4 teaspoons minced scallions
- 1 pound sushi-quality boneless, skinless salmon fillets
- ½ cup diced tomatoes
- ¼ cup wasabi powder
- ¼ cup rice or white vinegar
- 1 cup mayonnaise
- 2 teaspoons sesame oil
- 4 teaspoons soy sauce

blend to a smooth paste. Add the mayonnaise and blend well until smooth.

To assemble the dish

Remove the plates and molds from the refrigerator. Unmold the fish mixture by pressing down lightly on it while sliding the mold upward and off.

Place a few diced tomatoes on the top of the tower and sprinkle some of the minced scallions around the plate. Spoon 2 to 3 teaspoons of the wasabi mixture around the base of the tower. Drizzle ½ teaspoon of the sesame oil and 1 teaspoon of the soy sauce on and around the towers. Serve immediately.

Tomato-Mozzarella Club with Basil and Balsamic Syrup

Makes 4 sandwiches or 8 starters

Perfectly rustic simplicity makes this dish a great small starter or a staple for a full sandwich at lunch. It's one of my favorite quick and easy standbys; I eat as much as we serve. The key is great, ripe summer tomatoes and fresh, creamy mozzarella.

PREPARATION

To make the balsamic syrup

Balsamic syrup is a great addition to your kitchen; you may want to double the batch so you have plenty left over. It'll last for several months in your refrigerator.

Put all the vinegar in a nonreactive heavy-bottomed sauce pan. Bring it to a boil over medium heat, then reduce the heat to a simmer. Keep simmering until the vinegar is reduced by 80 percent. This may seem like a lot of vinegar to lose, but it's worth every drop. You don't need to buy expensive balsamic for this; any brand will do. There's no way to exactly measure the amount left in the pan unless you pour it back into the measuring cup; keep doing this until there's only approximately 3 ounces remaining. You can get a good indication of when the syrup is ready by tilting the saucepan; look for the vinegar to begin to "get legs," or lightly coat the back of a spoon.

When it's fully reduced, pour the syrup into a squeeze bottle or a sealable jar or bottle for easy use later. The syrup will thicken as it cools down and is perfect when served at room temperature. You'll notice that the acid has been boiled off; the syrup has a great sweet taste suitable for topping certain desserts.

INGREDIENTS

- 2 cups balsamic vinegar
- 2 ripe tomatoes
- 1 pound mozzarella
- 1 bunch fresh basil
- 12 slices white or whole wheat bread
- 4 teaspoons mayonnaise
- salt and pepper to taste

To assemble the clubs

Slice the tomatoes and mozzarella ¼ inch thick. Clean and dry the basil leaves. Toast all the bread and coat each slice with a thin smear of the mayo. Place 2 to 3 tomato slices (depending on their size) on 4 of the bread slices, and place a layer of basil leaves over the tomatoes. Lightly drizzle a little of the balsamic syrup over the tomatoes.

Place another slice of the bread on top of the first one. Cover the bread with sliced mozzarella, add another layer of the basil leaves, and another drizzle of the balsamic. Put another slice of the bread, mayo-side down, on top of the mozzarella.

You now have four club sandwiches of three layers each. Serve them as is or slice into four triangles. Place one triangle on each small plate; garnish with a little zigzag of the balsamic across the plate and a fresh basil leaf. Enjoy!

Wild Mushroom and Goat Cheese Tartlets

Makes 4 tarts

The earthy aroma and taste of these tarts provide a quintessential start to a cool autumn evening. The rustic shape of the free-form tart filled with creamy goat cheese and sautéed mushrooms helps set the tone for a great Pinot Noir or Burgundy. This is one of my favorite starters for a small party at home: You can prepare the tartlets well ahead of time and bake them at the last minute.

INGREDIENTS

2 9-inch piecrusts

4 ounces dry porcini mushrooms

¼ cup red wine

½ pound button mushrooms

½ pound shiitake mushrooms

4 teaspoons minced shallots

2 teaspoons minced garlic

2 tablespoons butter

¼ cup heavy cream

1½ teaspoons salt

¾ teaspoon black pepper

8 ounces goat cheese

PREPARATION

Making piecrust from scratch is certainly an option if you're comfortable with the process and have the time to do it. In lieu of making it, you may want to buy the refrigerated crusts from Pillsbury. I use them all the time and find them great in every way. Either way, begin with a 9-inch disk and roll it out to approximately 12 inches in diameter. Using a small plate or circular object that's 6 inches in diameter, cut the dough into two 6-inch disks. Repeat this process on the other crust to total four disks. Put them back in the refrigerator until you're ready to assemble the tarts.

Soak the porcinis in 1 quart of warm water for 15 minutes.

Remove the porcinis from the water, reserving ½ cup of the water. Dice the porcinis into ½-inch pieces. Clean the button mushrooms and slice them into ¼-inch pieces. Stem and clean the shiitakes and slice them into ¼-inch pieces.

Mince the shallots and garlic. In a 12-inch sauté pan, melt the butter over high heat. Add the shallots and garlic and sauté for 60 seconds.

Add the button and shiitake mushrooms and sauté for 4 minutes. Add the porcinis and sauté for 3 minutes. Add the wine to deglaze and cook for 2 minutes. Add the porcini water and reduce the heat to medium. Cook for 5 minutes, add the heavy cream, and continue to cook for 3 minutes longer.

Add the salt and pepper, stir to blend, and remove the pan from the heat to cool for at least 15 to 20 minutes.

Take the piecrust disks out of the refrigerator and place a heaping ¼ cup of the mushroom mixture in the center of each one. Put 1 ounce or 1 heaping tablespoon of the goat cheese on top of the mushroom filling, then fold the dough around the filling, leaving a 1-inch hole at the top (so you see the goat cheese popping through). Take the time to adjust the fold of the dough so the tartlets are all uniform.

Fifteen minutes before you plan to serve, place the tartlets on a baking sheet in a preheated 350-degree oven and bake for 12 to 15 minutes, or until the dough is golden brown.

I like to drizzle some balsamic syrup (see page 51) and a few drops of white truffle oil on the perimeter of the tarts; then I garnish by putting a sprig of Italian parsley in the center of the goat cheese. Serve immediately. I suggest a Pinot Noir as the perfect wine to complement this dish.

Doug's Coconut Tuna Ceviche

Makes 4 servings

Doug Rodriquez is a great friend and possibly the best Latino chef in the United States. The father of the Nuevo Latino explosion, he has had great success at his restaurants; his cookbooks reflect his style and outstanding food. This dish is one of my favorites from his repertoire. A hot summer night is the perfect occasion for this refreshing and addicting Honduran-inspired ceviche. The key—as in any ceviche or sushi-style dish—is impeccable fish. Be sure to request sushi quality when purchasing the tuna.

INGREDIENTS

1 14-ounce can unsweetened coconut milk

1 jalapeño, minced, with seeds

2 tablespoons finely minced fresh gingerroot

3 tablespoons Oriental fish sauce

1 tablespoon sugar

½ cup fresh lime juice

1 pound yellowfin, bluefin, or ahi tuna

¼ cup red onions, sliced thin in half moons

3 tablespoons minced fresh cilantro

¼ cup shaved coconut

2 tablespoons sliced scallions

PREPARATION

Place the coconut milk, jalapeño, gingerroot, fish sauce, sugar, and lime juice in a blender. Process till smooth and pureed.

Dice the tuna on a clean surface and keep chilled till you're ready to serve. Then toss the fish and the coconut mix in a bowl, and add the sliced onions and cilantro. Scoop equal amounts into a cool bowl or martini glass and sprinkle with the sliced scallions and shaved coconut. Serve immediately.

Oven-Roasted Portabella with Corn and Roasted Garlic Flan

Makes 4 servings

I first came up with this dish for a dinner party at home, and it was such a hit I knew it would end up on the Mist Grill menu someday. It did, and it still draws raves for its great contrast of tastes and textures. The presentation is unique and simple, making it exemplary of the classic rustic style at the Mist Grill.

INGREDIENTS

4 portabella mushroom caps

4 teaspoons olive oil

2 teaspoons balsamic vinegar

1 teaspoon salt

1½ cups corn kernels, fresh or frozen

1 head garlic (8–10 cloves)

1 cup heavy cream

½ cup milk

2 whole eggs

3 egg yolks

1 teaspoon salt

½ teaspoon black pepper

PREPARATION

A key to this dish is the size of the mushroom caps. You need caps whose inside diameter is slightly larger than the diameter of the ramekins you'll be making the flans in. The reason is that the mushroom cap will act as the cup for the flan when it's unmolded. So measure your ramekins before you shop and choose caps to fit.

Once you've figured all this out, begin by removing the stems of the mushrooms, then liberally brush the caps on both sides with the oil and vinegar, and sprinkle them equally with salt. Set them aside until you're ready to roast them.

Place the corn on an oiled baking sheet and spread it out in one layer. Roast the corn in a preheated 350-degree oven for approximately 20 minutes or until it just starts to brown at the edges. Remove and cool until you're ready to blend it into the flan mixture.

To roast the garlic, cut off the top of the bulb so the cloves are just exposed. Place this in the oven with the corn and roast for 20 minutes.

While the corn and garlic are roasting, make the flan mixture by combining the cream, milk, eggs, egg yolks, salt, and pepper. Whisk until fully blended.

Use some butter to coat the insides of the ramekins for easy removal of the flans later.

After the garlic is roasted, let it cool, then remove the cloves by squeezing each one out of its husk. Add the corn and the garlic to the flan mixture and blend well with a whisk.

continued next page

Ladle equal amounts of the flan mixture into each ramekin. Be sure to stir the mixture while you are ladling so you get an even amount of the corn and garlic dispersed in each ladleful.

Place the ramekins in a shallow roasting pan. Fill the pan with hot tap water until it comes halfway up the sides of the ramekins. Bake in the 350-degree oven for 25 to 35 minutes or until an inserted skewer come out clean.

Place the mushrooms on a baking sheet and roast them in the oven for 12 to 15 minutes.

To assemble the dish

Place a mushroom cap on each plate with the gill side facing up. Unmold the flans one at a time by running a knife around the edge of the ramekin, then turning the flan onto the mushroom cap. Done properly, the flan will be nesting inside the cap, with the sides of the mushroom just cradling the flan. Garnish with a nice plume or sprig of any available herb. Serve immediately.

SIDES, SPUDS, SOUPS, AND STUFF

Big plates sometimes depend on sides for additional fire. Innovative side dishes, simple and interesting soups, and the endless variations on the humble spud require some imagination to keep them from becoming starchy afterthoughts that detract from the stars of the show. The simple staples of the farm still sustain us. Potatoes, for instance, have been the basis of many diets for centuries; the classic peasant diet relied on ingredients that were easy to grow and could last in a cellar for months.

Today we are fortunate to have a wide array of interesting potato variations available: Yukon gold, red bliss, purple Peruvian, and large bakers from Idaho, to name just a few. At the Mist Grill we've been able to use these varieties to enhance our menu. While the potato may have long been served as a starchy necessity to fill out a meal, we aren't bound by that tradition today.

Such famous international dishes as cassoulet and paella were developed to use lesser-quality ingredients and represent a very rustic form of cookery. These dishes may have been created to use products that were less than appetizing, but when they were combined with key spices and stocks and cooked for extended periods of time, the result was hearty and nutritious meals that are deservedly world renowned.

We at the Mist Grill still use leftovers and scraps to create versions of many Old World classics, but the dishes have evolved to the point that they require fresh ingredients to provide the right balance of innovation and traditional rusticity. I believe that we all posses genetic memories, buried deep within, based on our ancestors' eating habits and the flavors and tastes they lived with. Maybe that's why certain dishes that we call comfort foods are so enjoyable: We connect to the past through the meals we eat today.

Killer Rösti Potatoes

Makes 6 to 8 servings

These classic potatoes originated in the kitchens of Switzerland and Germany, and I guess my German heritage is why I love them so much. They're extremely easy to prepare and can serve as a diverse side dish for almost any type of big plate.

The only challenge in making them the Mist Grill way is to have a mandolin. This tool is a great addition to any kitchen and can be purchased for $100 or less. The mandolin produces perfect fine julienne cuts, which are best for this dish. If one is not at hand or in the budget, you can use the largest hole on a standard box grater.

INGREDIENTS

3 large Idaho baking potatoes, peeled

1½ teaspoons salt

½ teaspoon black pepper

1 teaspoon dried rosemary *or* 2 teaspoons fresh

½ cup olive oil

PREPARATION

Preheat oven to 350 degrees.

Peel the potatoes and either run them through a mandolin or grate them on a box grater. If you're using a mandolin, set the blade for small julienne and adjust the flat blade so the cut produces a julienne that's a bit less than ⅛ inch square and about 2 inches long. Grate all the potatoes and sprinkle the salt, pepper, and rosemary over them. Mix well so they're evenly blended.

In a 10-inch nonstick sauté pan, add half the oil and heat to the point where the oil just begins to smoke. Very carefully add the potatoes to the pan all at once. Using a metal spatula, arrange the potatoes so they're evenly spread across the pan and level. Press them down so they're somewhat cakelike. The "cake" should not be more than 1 inch high. Cook for approximately 3 minutes or until they're golden brown on the bottom. Very carefully use the spatula to turn the entire cake over in the pan. Drizzle the remaining oil around the edge of the pan; you want the oil to reach the pan and not sit on top of the browned potatoes. Continue to cook until the bottom is also golden brown.

Remove the pan from the flame, carefully drain the residual oil, and place the pan in the oven. (Be sure its handle is ovenproof!) Bake the potatoes for 10 to 12 minutes, remove them from the pan, and slice them into equal triangles; you can get 6 to 8 portions per pan. Serve immediately.

Aged Cheddar and Heavy Cream Grits

Makes 4 large side-dish servings

INGREDIENTS

1 cup water

2 cups heavy cream

2 tablespoons unsalted butter

1 cup quick grits

1 cup grated Vermont Cheddar (aged 12–24 months)

¼ cup roughly diced scallions

There is nothing low fat about these grits. Still, they're the consummate rustic, country side dish for many of our main courses. Grits are usually associated with southern cooking, but I've no doubt the original millers at the Mist Grill once ate a similar dish 150 years ago right here in Vermont.

PREPARATION

Bring the water, cream, and butter to a simmer in a heavy-bottomed saucepan. Stir in the grits slowly and continue to stir until they're fully cooked. Read the instructions on the box to get an idea of the time; quick grits usually cook in about 5 to 8 minutes. Add the cheese and scallions and stir until the cheese is fully incorporated and melted. Season with salt and pepper to taste, if desired. Serve immediately.

Pan-Mashed Potatoes

Makes 6 to 8 servings

Our Sunday Supper concept—a family-style approach to dinner—started out as a test when we opened and has evolved to almost a cult status. Based on a blackboard menu, the evening features "leftovers" from the previous night's menu. We never know what we'll be serving until the very last minute, and we'll sometimes change the menu two or three times throughout the night as we run out of things and improvise on the fly. Diners love the spontaneity of the menu, and I love the way it forces the cooks to really get creative. Pan-Mashed Potatoes are one of the last-minute sides I threw together on a very busy night when I'd already run out of the other two side dishes.

There are basically no boundaries to making these potatoes; I've made them many times with all kind of things changed and added. Still, the following recipe is the original version.

INGREDIENTS

1 cup sweet potatoes

1 cup red-skinned potatoes

1 cup Yukon gold potatoes

3 tablespoons butter, divided

1 cup diced onions

2 tablespoons minced garlic

¼ cup diced red peppers

1 teaspoon salt

1 teaspoon pepper

1 tablespoon minced fresh rosemary

2 cups milk

1 cup crumbled Gorgonzola cheese

PREPARATION

Peel the sweet potatoes and dice them into ¾-inch cubes; leave the skin on the reds and Yukons and dice into ¾-inch cubes. Bring a large stockpot of water to a boil and cook all the potatoes until they're fork-tender. Drain and run cold water over them; set aside until you're ready to use them.

In a cast-iron skillet or large sauté pan (12-inch size), melt 1 tablespoon of the butter and add the onions, garlic, and red peppers. Sauté over high heat for 3 minutes, then add the precooked potatoes and sauté for 3 to 4 minutes longer. Add the salt, pepper, and rosemary; mix well. Then add the milk and remaining 2 tablespoons of butter and mix well. Reduce the heat to low and, using a hand masher, begin to mash the mixture until the potatoes are mashed but still chunky. Smooth the surface so they're level and patted down. Evenly sprinkle the Gorgonzola over the entire surface of the potatoes. Now you can either place the pan under a broiler until the cheese is bubbling and begins to brown, or bake it in a preheated 350-degree oven for 10 to 12 minutes. If you've used a cast-iron skillet, you can serve the potatoes at the table right out of the pan, using a trivet to protect your fine dining room wood!

Tomato Confit

Makes 4 servings

This recipe is both simple to prepare and a great way to transform a tomato into an interesting, tasty side dish. Served hot with a main course of fish or poultry, the confit provides a sweet and acidic balance; served at room temperature with sandwiches or salads, it becomes a refreshing side treat.

INGREDIENTS

8 plum tomatoes

2 cups olive oil

4 tablespoons salt

2 teaspoons cracked black pepper

8 garlic cloves

4 fresh rosemary sprigs

PREPARATION

Preheat oven to 300 degrees.

Place all the ingredients in a shallow roasting pan or ovenproof 9-by-11-by-2-inch cake pan. Mix to evenly disperse, and bake for 30 to 40 minutes. After 10 minutes, use a spoon to turn the tomatoes in the oil so they cook evenly. Repeat after another 10 minutes.

The tomatoes are done when the skin is wrinkled and beginning to split. Remove them from the oil and serve immediately, or refrigerate until you're ready to serve. Save the oil (removing the rosemary stems). This oil is great for use as a flavored oil for vinaigrettes, for dipping bread, or for sautéing.

Risotto Cakes with Asiago Gratin

Makes 6 to 8 cakes

Risotto is intimidating to many home cooks, and rightfully so. Making risotto requires patience and a certain level of endurance due to the need to stir continuously for 15 to 20 minutes. This recipe offers some forgiveness and a way to use the risotto if it doesn't work out to your expectations. The cakes rely on slightly overcooked, starchy risotto—and you can have them on hand, ready to cook off at a moment's notice.

PREPARATION

In a heavy-bottomed saucepan, melt the butter over medium heat. Add the onions and cook for 3 minutes; add the garlic and cook for 30 seconds. Add the rice and stir for 2 minutes, coating the rice with the butter. Using a ladle, add about 1 cup of the chicken stock while continuing to stir the rice with a wooden spoon. The stock will absorb quickly at first; as soon as it's incorporated, add another cup. Reduce the heat to low and continue to add stock in 4- to 6-ounce increments, stirring all the while, until all the stock is incorporated. This will take approximately 15 to 20 minutes. Do not rush the process. To see if the rice is done, squeeze a grain; it should mash with some resistance, and the center of the kernel should still be a bit firm. Add the cream, 1 cup of the Asiago, the sage, salt, and pepper. Blend uniformly.

You can serve the risotto as is; garnish with the remaining cheese.

To make the cakes, pour the risotto into a roasting pan and quickly smooth it until it's

INGREDIENTS

- 2 tablespoons butter
- ½ cup ¼-inch-dice onions
- 1 tablespoon minced garlic
- 1 cup arborio rice
- 3 cups chicken stock
- ½ cup heavy cream
- 1½ cups grated Asiago cheese
- 2 tablespoons minced fresh sage *or* 1 tablespoon dried
- 1 teaspoon salt
- ½ teaspoon black pepper

level. Try to size the pan so the risotto fills it to about 1 inch high. Cool the risotto for 15 to 20 minutes, then cover and refrigerate for at least 2 or 3 hours.

When you're ready to serve, cut the risotto into 3- to 4-inch squares.

Add enough olive oil to a large sauté pan to sufficiently coat the bottom. Heat the oil to approximately 350 degrees (below the smoke point). Place the cakes in the pan and cook for 3 minutes per side or until golden brown and crisp.

Place the cakes on a baking sheet and evenly sprinkle the remaining Asiago over them. You can either bake the cakes at 350 degrees for about 8 minutes, or place them under a broiler to melt and slightly brown the cheese. Serve immediately with any main-course dish.

Smoky and Spicy Black Beans

Makes 8 to 10 servings

I love traditional baked beans, but I also love the spice and smoke from chipotle peppers. I created this dish to be paired with south-of-the-border-style foods, and especially with barbecued chicken or ribs. You can expect a drop of sweat on the brow from this dish, but if you're looking for less heat, simply reduce the amount of chipotles. This dish can be made very quickly with canned beans, but if you have the time to soak and cook the dry beans, go ahead and do so.

INGREDIENTS

½ pound smoked bacon, diced

1 cup diced green bell peppers

4 chipotle peppers (canned in adobo), minced

1 cup diced onions

2 cups chicken stock

3 cans (16 ounces each) black beans, undrained

3 tablespoons chili powder

1 tablespoon cumin powder

¼ cup brown sugar

1½ teaspoons salt

¼ cup cider vinegar

4 teaspoons minced fresh cilantro (for garnish)

¼ cup sour cream (for garnish)

PREPARATION

Add enough vegetable oil to a medium to large saucepot to coat the bottom of the pot. Add the diced bacon and cook for 4 to 5 minutes, until the bacon fat is rendered and the bacon is browned. Add the peppers and onions and cook for 3 to 4 minutes.

Add the chicken stock and beans with all the juice from the cans. Add all the other ingredients except the vinegar and garnishes.

Reduce the heat to low and simmer the mixture for 20 minutes. Add the vinegar, stir in, and cook for 3 minutes.

The beans can be served immediately, topped with 1 tablespoon of the cilantro and the sour cream. The beans will keep for 3 to 4 days under refrigeration; you'll find that they reach their optimal flavor at days 2 and 3, after the flavors have a chance to marry.

Bea's Firecracker Apple Fritters

Makes 10 to 12 fritters

My mother, Beatrice, makes the greatest apple fritters. We usually found them on the table with pan-fried pork chops. Over the years I've tried to duplicate them, but I've never gotten them exactly right. So instead I customized them, adding another element to make them a bit more unusual: jalapeños. Still, the inspiration for these tasty little fritters must be credited to Mom. A huge believer in making life easy in the kitchen, she uses Bisquick in this recipe—one of the original convenience foods and still one of the best.

INGREDIENTS

2 cups Bisquick

2 eggs

1¼ cups milk

2 medium apples

1 tablespoon minced jalapeños

½ teaspoon salt

½ cup canola oil

PREPARATION

Mix the Bisquick, eggs, and milk. Grate the apples with the skin on and add them directly to the batter. Add the diced jalapeños and salt and blend well. The fritters are only good for several minutes after frying, so wait until you're ready to serve them before cooking.

Heat the oil in a large cast-iron skillet or sauté pan. The oil should be approximately 350 degrees. To test its temperature, drop a small amount of the mixture into the pan. It should immediately begin to fry but not burn. Most rangetops should be set at medium to reach this temperature range.

Scoop out about 2 ounces (3 tablespoons) of the mixture and place it in the pan. Quickly spread the mixture out so the fritter is 2 to 3 inches across. You can fit 4 to 6 fritters in the pan at once, depending on the size of your skillet. Cook for about 60 seconds, then carefully turn them over and cook for an additional 60 to 90 seconds. Remove from the pan and drain on paper towels for 10 to 20 seconds. Serve immediately.

Grilled Ratatouille

Makes 4 to 6 servings

Growing up, I always thought ratatouille represented a real culinary specialty. It had that cool French name; I felt like I was cooking with style. It is, however, a very simple dish that truly represents the rustic side of French food. I've made about a million versions of ratatouille over the years, most recently a grilled version that elevates the dish to new levels of flavor and texture.

It's still an easy dish to prepare, though pre-grilling the vegetables does require some extra attention to detail.

INGREDIENTS

1 eggplant

2 zucchini

2 yellow squash

1 red onion

1 red pepper

1 green pepper

¼ cup olive oil

3 tablespoons salt-and-pepper blend (80:20 ratio)

8 plum tomatoes

5 garlic cloves, minced

¼ cup white wine

1 can (8–10 ounces) tomato paste

2 tablespoons fine herb blend

PREPARATION

Cut the eggplant into ½-inch-thick circles. Cut the zucchini and squash into ½-inch-thick planks. Cut the onion into ½-inch-thick circles. Quarter the peppers and remove the seeds and stems. Toss all of the vegetables in a bowl with the oil and salt-and-pepper blend.

On a preheated charcoal grill, begin to grill the vegetables (reserving the bowl of oil). Grill them on both sides until slightly charred. Continue until all are done. Toss the tomatoes in the oil and salt-and-pepper blend and grill them whole until they're blistered and just about to burst. Let all the vegetables cool, then cut them all into 1-inch cubes.

Coat the bottom of a large sauté pan with oil and add all the vegetables and garlic cloves. Sauté for about 2 minutes. Add the white wine and tomato paste and blend well. Reduce the heat to low and add the fine herb blend. Simmer for 10 minutes and serve immediately.

Israeli Couscous Risotto-Style

Makes 6 to 8 servings

Israeli Couscous comes in large pearls; they're about the size of BB gun pellets. I fell in love with this the first time I cooked it and then again when I ate it. The couscous has a great texture—much better than that of the standard small pearls—along with a terrific nutty, toasted flavor. It also lends itself to some nontraditional cooking methods, such as risotto-style. The ultimate pairing is with lamb, especially if you use a Middle Eastern flair with the seasonings—maybe curry, cinnamon, or fenugreek. It's also very forgiving in the way it cooks and can be customized with myriad added ingredients.

This is the simplest version, so use your imagination with things you can blend in! Israeli couscous is growing more and more popular and can be found in many stores.

INGREDIENTS

2 tablespoons butter

½ cup finely diced onions

2 cups Israeli couscous

1 quart chicken stock

1 tablespoon curry powder

1 teaspoon cinnamon

3 tablespoons minced fresh parsley

1 tablespoon salt

1 teaspoon pepper

PREPARATION

In a large heavy-bottomed saucepan, melt the butter over medium heat. Add the onions and sauté for 3 minutes. Add the couscous and sauté for 2 minutes while stirring well. Begin to add the chicken stock ½ cup at a time, stirring constantly. Continue to add the stock as the pearls absorb it; this will take about 10 minutes from start to finish. The couscous is done when the pearls are tender yet slightly al dente. Add the remaining ingredients and blend well. Serve immediately. You can also keep this in the refrigerator; add some stock before reheating and serving to hydrate it again.

Lobster Latté

Makes 8 lattés

This "soup" plays to our whimsy—yet in a country way. Its basc is an unrefined bisque, which makes it rustic and hearty. The latté component comes in when you top the soup with both foamed and steamed milk. The presentation is a wonderful way to show off a bit with an easy and functional garnish. We serve it in traditional latté bowls, but regular old coffee mugs look great, too. Please note that you need an espresso or cappuccino machine to make the foam and steam the milk. If you don't have one you can omit the foam, or replace it with unsweetened whipped cream.

INGREDIENTS

2 lobsters, 1 pound each

1 cup butter

½ cup minced onions

2 tablespoons minced garlic

½ cup flour

2 cups heavy cream

1 can (8–10 ounces) tomato paste

1 teaspoon nutmeg

salt and pepper to taste

2 cups 2 percent milk

PREPARATION

Steam the lobsters in a large covered stockpot for about 8 minutes. Chill immediately, then remove every speck of meat; don't discard any of the shells. Chop the lobster meat into ½-inch chunks and chill until you're ready to use it.

Put all the lobster shells in a large stockpot and add 3 quarts of water. Bring the pot to a boil and then reduce the heat to a simmer and cook for 45 minutes. Strain the stock through a fine-mesh strainer and discard the shells. You'll need 2 quarts of the lobster stock for this recipe.

In a heavy-bottomed saucepot, melt the butter over a medium flame and add the onions and garlic. Cook for 3 minutes, then start to slowly add the flour while stirring well. When all the flour is incorporated, continue to cook the roux for approximately 3 minutes or until it just begins to smell nutty and is very lightly browned. Quickly whisk in the lobster stock, whisking until all the roux is dissolved.

Reduce the heat to low and simmer for 15 minutes. Add all the remaining ingredients except the lobster and the milk. Continue to cook for approximately 8 to 10 minutes, or until the soup easily coats the back of a spoon.

You can keep the soup warm until you're ready to serve, or refrigerate it and reheat it over a low flame, stirring regularly.

72

To serve the lattés

Place the 2 percent milk in the steam cup and make foam as you would for a cappuccino. Place an equal amount of the chopped lobster meat in the bottom of each bowl or mug. Immediately pour in the *hot* soup to fill each bowl or mug about three-quarters of the way up the sides. Spoon the foamed milk onto the tops of each serving, then pour about 2 tablespoons of the steamed milk into it as well. Sprinkle a dusting of nutmeg or black pepper atop the foam and serve immediately.

Cream of Portabella

Makes 6 to 8 servings

Soups are commonly thought of as classic comfort foods—and this one truly fits the bill. Our menu at the Mist Grill changes every six weeks, but this soup has remained on almost every menu during the appropriate seasons. It's rich, hearty, and delicious!

INGREDIENTS

½ cup butter, divided

¼ cup flour

6 large portabella caps

6 ounces bacon, diced

½ cup minced onions

3 tablespoons minced garlic

2 cups water

1 cup milk

1 cup heavy cream

2 teaspoons salt

1 teaspoon black pepper

PREPARATION

Melt ¼ cup of the butter in a heavy saucepan. Slowly add the flour and mix well. Cook the roux, stirring constantly, until the flour begins to turn to a very light brown or blond color. Remove from the heat and set aside until later.

Remove the stems from the mushrooms and finely dice them. Remove the gills from the undersides of the caps by using a spoon to scrape them out. (This prevents the soup from getting too dark or muddy looking from the gills' black color.) Dice the caps into ¼-inch size.

In a heavy-bottomed saucepot, cook the bacon over medium heat until the fat is rendered and it just begins to brown. Add the onions and garlic and continue to cook until the onions are translucent and browning at the edges. Add the remaining butter and the diced stems and cook for 4 minutes. Add the diced portabellas and cook for 5 minutes. Add the water, milk, and cream and simmer over medium heat for 20 minutes.

Whisk in the roux and blend well. Continue to cook for 5 minutes. Season with salt and pepper; if the soup has gotten too thick, you can add a little more cream or milk. As an added touch during the winter months, we offer a splash of sherry to pour into the soup just as it's served.

Mushroom Cappuccino

Makes 12 servings

This variation on Cream of Portabella soup is similar to Lobster Latté (see page 72) in its presentation—a highlight of any dinner. We serve it in smaller cups and garnish with only foamed milk, not steamed.

PREPARATION

Follow the recipe for Cream of Portabella soup on page 74. Let the soup cool enough for safe handling in a blender or food processor, then puree it in either machine until it's smooth. Pour it into a saucepan and heat over low heat until it's simmering.

Using your trusty espresso or cappuccino machine, foam approximately 4 ounces of 2 percent milk. Ladle about 6 ounces of the soup into each cup and top with a generous amount of the foamed milk. Sprinkle some white pepper atop the foam and serve immediately.

Corn Chowder with Shrimp and Green Chilies

Makes 6 to 8 servings

Latino in origin, this recipe is not chowder in the traditional sense. My friend Doug Rodriquez makes a similar soup called *chupes* ("chowder" in Spanish). I've played with making my own *chupes;* here's the version that has evolved.

PREPARATION

Begin by peeling the shrimp and deveining and dicing them into ¼-inch size. Chill until you're ready to use them.

Place all the shrimp shells in a large saucepan and cover with 3 quarts of water. Bring to a boil, then reduce the heat to medium and cook for 20 minutes. Strain the stock and discard the shells. You'll need 1 quart of stock for this recipe.

Add enough oil to a large stockpot to coat the bottom of the pot. Over medium heat, add the onions, garlic, and celery. Sauté for 4 minutes. Add the jalapeños, turmeric, and potatoes and cook for 3 minutes. Add the shrimp stock and the coconut milk and simmer for 15 minutes. Add the tomatoes and saffron and cook for 5 min-utes. Stir the diced shrimp into the soup; they'll cook almost instantly, so wait until just before serving to add them. Cook for 2 minutes, then add the cilantro and stir. Serve immediately.

You can enhance the flavor of the shrimp stock by using a shrimp stock base, available at ChefEx.net.

INGREDIENTS

1 pound shrimp (21–25 count per pound)

½ cup diced onions

2 tablespoons minced garlic

½ cup diced celery

4 jalapeños, minced, with seeds

1 teaspoon turmeric powder

2 cups peeled, diced potatoes

2 14-ounce cans unsweetened coconut milk

1 cup diced tomatoes

15–20 saffron threads

3 tablespoons minced fresh cilantro

Roasted Tomato, White Bean, and Spinach Soup

Makes 10 to 12 servings

The epitome of rustic and hearty, this soup finds its way onto the menu in the dead of winter. I suggest making a large batch— enough for several meals. I love having this soup for lunch with just a slice of warm sourdough bread or a good crusty chunk of French bread.

PREPARATION

Rinse the beans and check for any small pebbles; stones are a bit too rustic! Soak the beans for at least 4 hours in a large stockpot with 3 quarts of water. Bring the pot to a boil, then reduce the heat to a simmer and cook for approximately 45 to 60 minutes, or until the beans are tender to the tooth. Drain the liquid, reserving 1 cup of it.

While the beans are cooking, split the tomatoes in half lengthwise and place them cut-side up on a baking sheet. Lightly salt and pepper them, and sprinkle them with a small amount of the basil. In a preheated 350-degree oven, bake them for 20 to 25 minutes, or until they're beginning to brown and dry out. Remove them from the oven and let them cool.

In a large stockpot, add the olive oil and sauté the diced vegetables and garlic over high heat for 4 to 5 minutes or until well browned.

Add the chicken stock and the cooked beans to the pot and reduce the heat to medium. Cook the beans for 20 minutes and add the remaining basil, oregano, and pepper.

INGREDIENTS

- 1 pound dried white beans (European or soldier)
- 12 plum tomatoes
- 3 tablespoons dried basil, divided
- ¼ cup olive oil
- ½ cup finely diced celery
- ½ cup finely diced carrots
- ½ cup finely diced onions
- 3 tablespoons minced garlic
- 2 quarts chicken stock
- 1 tablespoon dried oregano
- 1 tablespoon black pepper
- salt to taste
- 1 12-ounce bag spinach, stemmed

(A tablespoon may sound like a lot of pepper, but the soup should have a deep pepper kick.) Use some of the reserved bean juice to adjust the flavor and consistency, if needed. Adjust the seasonings to taste.

When you're ready to serve the soup, warm the tomatoes in the oven for 5 minutes. Place approximately 5 to 6 spinach leaves in the bottom of each bowl, then 4 tomatoes; ladle the soup into the bowl. Use a fork to help wilt the spinach and pull some of the green up through the soup.

Creamy Chipotle Polenta

Makes 6 to 8 servings

We love to use corn when it's fresh, and this version of polenta originated when we harvested an abundance of corn one year. The fresh, sweet kernels add a great texture and a taste of summer in Vermont. We serve this with our barbecued ribs and chicken, especially Black Cherry and Chipotle Baby Back Ribs (see page 94).

INGREDIENTS

6–8 ears corn (enough for 2 cups fresh corn kernels)

3 cups milk

3 cups water

4–5 chipotles (canned in adobo), minced

2 cups cornmeal

1 cup shredded Monterey jack cheese

2 tablespoons minced fresh cilantro

1½ –3 teaspoons salt (taste while blending)

PREPARATION

Shuck the corn and cook the ears in boiling water for 3 minutes. Remove and immediately chill under cold water. Cut the kernels off the cobs and reserve.

In a heavy-bottomed saucepan, bring the milk, water, and chipotles to a boil. Reduce the heat to medium and gradually stir in the cornmeal until it's very well blended.

Cook for approximately 12 to 15 minutes, stirring constantly.

When the polenta is creamy and smooth, add the corn kernels and mix well. Let the corn cook for 3 minutes, then add the shredded cheese. Continue to cook while stirring for 2 to 3 minutes. Blend in the cilantro, add salt to taste, and serve immediately.

VARIATION

You can also turn this polenta into griddle cakes. Pour the polenta into a jelly roll pan, let it cool, and cut it into squares. Add enough oil to a heavy-bottomed skillet to cover by approximately ⅛ inch. Heat over medium heat until the oil will crisp the polenta quickly. Place the cakes in the pan and cook until deep golden brown on both sides.

Summer Fair "Dipped" Corn on the Cob

Makes 12 ears

This may be my favorite way to devour fresh summer corn on the cob. I was introduced to it by a street vendor in the barrio section of Milwaukee. (No, Wisconsin isn't the first place you think of for Latino street food, but there's a very healthy population of Latin Americans there.) The dish is very easy and sure to be the hit of your summer barbecue!

INGREDIENTS

1 cup mayonnaise

2 tablespoons chili powder

1 teaspoon garlic salt

½ teaspoon cumin powder

2 cups grated Manchego or Asiago cheese

12 ears fresh corn

PREPARATION

Mix the mayonnaise and spices well and set aside until you're ready to use. Place the grated cheese in a dish or roasting pan. It should be grated very fine—as fine as coarse sand; use a food processor for best results.

In a large stockpot, bring to a boil enough water to fully cover the corn. Add the corn and cook for 6 to 8 minutes, or until the corn is cooked but still firm and crunchy.

Using either cob holders or a candy apple skewer, skewer the corn through the bottom of the cob so you can hold the ear by the stick. Quickly paint the ear with a liberal amount of the seasoned mayonnaise using a pastry brush. Be sure to coat the entire cob. Roll the painted cob in the grated cheese and serve immediately. Be prepared for your guests to request a second or third serving!

Robin's "I Invented It" Mac and Cheese

Makes 6 servings

My partner, Robin, is an accomplished chef, and she and I always seem to be jokingly bickering over who "invented" a particular dish. She's always said that my mac and cheese is terrible and hers is the best—and indeed, I must give Robin her due on this recipe. No, she didn't actually invent mac and cheese, but we'll let her think she did.

Good old mac and cheese is one of those dishes that's timeless and represents the height of comfort food, and using couscous instead of macaroni gives it a whole new texture dimension. We love to serve this as a rib-sticking side dish on our Sunday Supper menus.

INGREDIENTS

1 pound Israeli couscous

¼ cup butter

¼ cup minced onions

¼ cup flour

1 teaspoon dry mustard

¼ teaspoon white pepper

3½ cups milk

2 cups shredded sharp Vermont Cheddar cheese

½ cup grated Parmesan cheese

1 cup buttered bread crumbs

PREPARATION

Preheat oven to 350 degrees.

Bring a large stockpot full of water to a boil and cook the couscous for 6 to 8 minutes, or until just al dente. Drain and rinse the couscous under cool water.

In a large saucepan, melt the butter and sauté the onions for 4 minutes. Add the flour, mustard, and pepper. Cook the roux over medium heat until it just begins to brown.

Add the milk and whisk until the mixture is completely smooth, with no lumps. Reduce the heat to low and continue whisking until the sauce thickens. Add the cheeses and stir until melted and smooth. Add the couscous and combine well. Pour the mix into a baking dish and cover the top with the bread crumbs. Bake for 15 to 20 minutes.

Summer Pea Salad

Makes 6 to 8 servings

I first made this at my first restaurant, the Terrace on the Plaza in Locust Valley, New York. It was an immediate hit and became a signature salad during the summer months. The sweetness of the peas combined with the other ingredients provides a soothing and tasty side dish that can be served with anything at all! My mother also fell in love with it and has given the recipe to literally a hundred of her friends, so here's the official Summer Pea Salad.

INGREDIENTS

8 strips bacon

1 pound frozen peas

¾ cup mayonnaise

½ cup plain yogurt

¼ cup Dijon mustard

½ cup red wine vinegar

1 teaspoon salt

½ teaspoon black pepper

3 tomatoes, diced

1 cup diced red onions

PREPARATION

Cook the bacon and dice it into ¼-inch pieces. Rinse the peas in a strainer under warm water and drain well. In a mixing bowl, combine the mayonnaise, yogurt, Dijon mustard, vinegar, salt, and pepper, whisking well until smooth. Add the diced tomatoes, onions, and peas and toss. Add the bacon just before serving so it stays crunchy. (You can omit the bacon for a meatless dish, but the bacon gives a great smoky, salty flavor.) Serve immediately. The salad will keep overnight, but the peas will start to discolor within a day.

Thai Coleslaw

Makes 6 to 8 servings

I love the fresh flavors of Thai food. This easy version of coleslaw complements many dishes, especially fish or chicken off the grill.

PREPARATION

Shred the cabbage. In a large bowl, combine it with all the other vegetables, the mango, and the cilantro. Toss well.

Combine all the remaining ingredients in a bowl and whisk well until smooth and slightly emulsified. Add the dressing to the slaw and toss well. Let it sit refrigerated for 1 to 2 hours, then toss again and serve.

INGREDIENTS

2 heads Napa cabbage

1 cup thin-shaved red onions

1 red pepper, finely julienned

1 jalapeño pepper, minced, without seeds

½ cup diced mango

¼ cup minced fresh cilantro

¾ cup canola oil

¼ cup sesame oil

¼ cup soy sauce

¼ cup honey

3 tablespoons sesame seeds

2 teaspoons dry mustard

Steve's Red Spud Salad with Dijon Dressing

Makes 8 servings

I love potato salad, and I've made millions of pounds of this classic country version. It gets served during summer on many plates, even the fancy dinners when paired with our ribeye.

PREPARATION

Place the potatoes in a large stockpot and cover with water. Bring to a boil and cook for 8 to 10 minutes or until they're just fork-tender. Drain and run cool water to quickly chill. Cut the potatoes into sixths or eighths, depending on their size; you should end up with wedges of about ¾ inch. Add the celery and onions.

In another bowl, combine all the other ingredients and whisk well. Toss the dressing with the potato mix and blend well to coat evenly. Chill the potato salad for at least 2 hours to let the potatoes soak up some of the dressing.

INGREDIENTS

16 red-skinned potatoes

1 cup diced celery

1 cup diced red onions

1½ cups mayonnaise

3 tablespoons balsamic vinegar

¼ cup red wine vinegar

¼ cup coarse-grained Dijon mustard

2 teaspoons salt

1 teaspoon black pepper

BIG PLATES

Our Vermont landscape—farms blending into deep green forests, crystal lakes reflecting the clear blue sky, fiery autumn leaves illuminating the mountains, pristine blankets of white snow—provides us with endless inspiration to mirror nature's beauty in our food. If rustic means simple, country, and bucolic, then Vermont is the quintessential example of rusticity.

We feel spoiled sometimes by the natural wonders that surround us in Vermont, and we at the Mist Grill know that we have an advantage over many urban restaurants for this reason alone. This all may sound a little mushy coming from a chef, but your surroundings help create your cooking style as much as they do your state of mind, and can influence how you consider an ingredient or design a dish. If all you can see from your kitchen are gray cement blocks or brick walls, it's difficult to draw inspiration from nature.

While it's nothing like our New England landscape, one recent presentation trend supplies a certain kind of drama that we wholeheartedly encourage: over-sized plates and bowls. Think of each one as a canvas on which to showcase the food as well as helping various components stand out. There's enough space that you needn't bunch any foods on top of each other. I'm sure you've seen "vertical dishes" in restaurants—foods piled so high, the plate looks like what a hungry man brings back from an all-you-can-eat buffet table. All those different colors, textures, and flavors become one big mess. But with a big plate, you have a large area to "paint" on.

Still, just because the plate is big doesn't mean it has to be filled. For example, a perfect yet small medallion of lamb served on a disk of polenta with just a drizzle of sauce surrounding it, and most of the plate left open, can be beautiful. The openness of the plate draws your eye to its center. In my opinion, some of the most spontaneous artwork occurs on 12-inch white plates, blending the beautiful colors of Mother Nature's best ingredients. Food presented in a simple, unadorned fashion on a pristine white plate can be a living example of nature's bounty, enhanced by the cook's artful hand.

On the Mist Grill menu the main courses are referred to as big plates, not only because the food is presented on large surfaces, but also because it's here that the really big flavors take over. I love to serve dishes bold in flavor (especially paired with robust wines and local boutique beers). Few guests leave the

Mist Grill wondering why "garlic" or "chili" was found on the list of a dish's ingredients. Big flavor will only stay that way if you don't dilute your ingredients with too many others. It's a simple concept, but one easily forgotten. All too often, food becomes a confusing or homogeneous blend of flavors that either neutralize one another—or turn out just plain bad!

To deliver big and bold flavors successfully, focus on the main flavors in the dish and let them do their job. The old adage "Less is more" applies here.

Our big plate recipes are designed to be fun and easy and will provide a great assortment of options and ideas to expand on. Remember, your influence on the dishes is what will make them yours! Don't hesitate to experiment with alternative ingredients or cooking methods. Meat and fish, for instance, can take on different aspects when roasted or grilled or sautéed. Restaurants reinvent their foods all the time; you too should feel free to interchange ideas, ingredients, and methods.

We hope that our big plates at the Mist Grill reflect the sights, aromas, and textures of life in rural Vermont. When you're preparing to cook any of these recipes, try thinking about the Vermont landscape (unless, of course, you're already there), or any lovely rural setting. The aromas of fresh rosemary can place you in the middle of a pine forest; smoky bacon will conjure up a cold winter breakfast before a morning of chores; a skillet of corn bread with warm maple syrup provides images of spring's maple sugaring; fresh-picked garden vegetables let you almost smell summer's fresh-cut grass and tomato vines.

Indeed, we can experience food with all of our senses—not just our taste buds! The emotional aspect of food is very powerful, and I believe that our food at the Mist Grill blends this emotional connection with our surroundings, which helps make each dish special in more ways than one.

Sea Salt and Sage Crusted Chicken with Pearl Onion Gravy and Robin's Mac and Cheese

Makes 4 servings

At the Mist Grill we always have a chicken dish on the menu; this particular recipe has often stayed on the menu while other dishes change—because it's so good. It delivers the consummate feeling of warmth and comfort both when you smell it cooking and when you take the first bite.

PREPARATION

Preheat oven to 350 degrees.

Evenly coat the skin sides of the chicken breasts with 1 teaspoon of the salt and ½ teaspoon of the sage. Let them sit refrigerated for 1 hour.

Boil some water in a small saucepan and blanch the pearl onions for 3 minutes. Rinse to cool, and then peel off the onion skins.

For the chicken stock, you can use a prepared stock or concentrate. I love the Roasted Chicken Demi-Glace from Demi-Glace Gold. Or you can make a scratch stock (see page 159).

In a saucepan, make a roux by melting the butter and slowly whisking in the flour. Cook over low heat while stirring for approximately 5 minutes or until very lightly browned. Set aside.

In another saucepan, add enough oil to coat the pan and add the onions and garlic. Sauté for 3 to 4 minutes, until the onions begin to brown. Add the chicken stock, reduce the heat to medium, and simmer for 20 minutes. Whisk in the roux and blend until the mixture is smooth and begins to thicken. Add the cream and black pepper and simmer for 10 minutes.

In a large sauté pan, heat the canola oil to

INGREDIENTS

4 bone-in chicken breasts

4 teaspoons sea salt *or* kosher salt, divided

2 teaspoons rubbed dried sage, divided

1 cup fresh pearl onions

3 cups chicken stock

2 tablespoons butter

2 tablespoons flour

1 tablespoon minced garlic

½ cup heavy cream

½ teaspoon black pepper

1 tablespoon canola oil

4 cups Robin's Mac and Cheese (see page 80)

just below the smoke point and place the chicken breast skin-side down. Cook for approximately 4 minutes, until the skin is well browned. Turn the breasts and cook for 4 more minutes. Place the sauté pan in the oven and bake for 6 to 8 minutes.

Adjust the seasonings of the gravy if needed with some salt or some extra sage.

To serve the dish

Place a cup of the mac and cheese on the center of the plate. Slice the chicken across the breast into 4 even slices. Arrange these slices around the mound of mac and cheese, then ladle about 6 tablespoons of the gravy around and on the chicken. Garnish with a sprig of fresh herb in the center of the macaroni. Serve immediately.

Oven-Roasted Cod with Clam Chowder Broth

Makes 4 servings

In my opinion, this dish is New England at its finest! Both cod and clam chowder appeared in early cookbooks, and this recipe captures the essence of their Old World flavors in an updated form. The only problem with the dish is that it's so popular we have a hard time getting enough cod to last the weekend.

PREPARATION

In stock pot, cook the bacon until it just begins to brown. Add the vegetables and cook for 6 to 8 minutes over medium heat. Add the clam juice, reduce the heat to low, and simmer for 20 minutes. Add the clams and cream and simmer for 10 minutes. Add half the salt and pepper, adjusting to taste if needed. The clam chowder is not meant to be thick, but rather more brothlike.

Preheat oven to 350 degrees. In a sauté pan, melt the butter over high heat. Season both sides of the fish with the remaining salt and pepper, and sear both sides in the butter until golden brown. Then bake the fish for 6 minutes, or until just firm to the touch. Place the sliced French bread in the oven to warm.

INGREDIENTS

6 strips bacon, diced

½ cup diced celery

½ cup diced onions

1 cup diced red-skinned potatoes

¼ cup minced red pepper

1 quart clam juice

1 can (16 ounces) chopped clams

2 cups heavy cream

4 teaspoons salt

2 teaspoons black pepper

2 tablespoons butter

4 fresh cod fillets, 6–8 ounces each

4 slices (3 inches long by 1 inch thick) French bread

Place a slice of the bread in the center of each large soup bowl, top it with a cod fillet, and then ladle 4 to 6 ounces of the chowder broth into the bowl. Sprinkle some finely chopped parsley around the bowl and serve immediately.

Grilled Ribeye of Beef with Blue Cheese Butter and Tomato Cruda

Makes 4 servings

The ribeye we serve at the Mist Grill changes with the seasons, but it's always on the menu—the only item that stays on every time, due to its popularity. We get great beef and we dry-age it for at least 14 days. Dry-aging isn't really practical at home, however; you have to age a whole cut of the beef, and that weighs about 20 pounds. In lieu of this, be sure to ask for the best beef available. Prime is worth the extra cost. We always grill our steaks and suggest that they be cooked medium rare for optimal taste and texture. No matter what we pair with the steak, we always make sure that the beef is highlighted. This particular version of ribeye is one of my favorites: Simple to prepare, it's full of bold flavor from the Blue Cheese Butter. It screams for a really big Cabernet or Syrah!

INGREDIENTS

- 4 well-trimmed ribeye steaks, 12 ounces each
- 1 cup butter
- 8 ounces blue cheese
- 1 tablespoon cracked black pepper
- 2 tablespoons lemon juice
- ¼ cup finely snipped chives
- 1 pint cherry tomatoes
- 2 tablespoons chopped fresh basil
- ½ teaspoon salt
- ¼ teaspoon black pepper
- 2 tablespoons olive oil
- 1 tablespoon minced garlic
- 1 tablespoon balsamic vinegar

PREPARATION

Season the steaks on both sides with a liberal amount of salt and pepper. Keep chilled until you're ready to grill.

In a mixing bowl, add the butter and blue cheese and let soften. You can use a mixer to cream the two, or use a large fork to blend them together. Add the cracked pepper, lemon juice, and chives. Blend well and keep at room temperature until ready to use. The butter will keep for 2 to 3 days in the refrigerator if needed.

To make the Tomato Cruda, cut the cherry tomatoes in half and place them in a bowl. Add the basil, salt, pepper, olive oil, garlic, and balsamic vinegar and toss well. Prepare this at least 1 to 2 hours before serving.

When you're ready to serve, on a preheated charcoal grill, place the steaks all at a 45-degree

continued next page

angle pointing right. Grill for 2 minutes, then switch the position of the steaks to the opposite 45-degree angle pointing left. This will provide the traditional diamond grill marking.

Cook for 2 minutes, then flip the steaks over and continue to cook for 2 to 3 minutes. The art of cooking steaks to the right doneness is learned from cooking a lot of steaks. The best way to test a steak is by pressing down on the meat. Try it when it's raw; it'll easily yield to the pressure and feel mushy and soft. The opposite extreme is a well-done steak. When you press down on this, it'll be very firm and rigid. Medium rare to medium should feel right between raw and well done when pressure is applied. It's also important to account for the carryover cooking time once a steak is off the grill. The meat will continue to cook for about 60 seconds, then it'll begin to "relax" and juices will start to flow from it. So plan on undercooking slightly. The best rule to remember is that you can always cook the beef a bit more, but you can't undo a well-done steak!

When the steak is done, place a mound of the Tomato Cruda on the center of the plate. Place the steak halfway on the tomatoes, then put 1 heaping tablespoon of the Blue Cheese Butter on the steak. Serve immediately.

We often serve Steve's Red Spud Salad (see page 83) as the starch with this version of ribeyes.

Dave Burke's Roasted Pork Shank with Poppy Seed Kraut

Makes 4 servings

Dave Burke is one of the finest and most inventive chefs in the United States. Known for his whimsy, Dave constantly comes up with clever twists on old classics. He refers to this cut of pork as the Flintstones portion, and it is!

Technically, these cuts are known as foreshanks, and your butcher or meat department will require some lead time to get them for you. They're well worth the extra effort, though. Each cut of the shank is about 10 to 12 inches long and weighs about 2 pounds.

INGREDIENTS

2 cups sugar

2 cups kosher salt

4 pork shanks

2 cups apple cider

1 head cabbage

¼ cup apple cider vinegar

1½ teaspoons salt

½ teaspoon white pepper

3 tablespoons white pepper

PREPARATION

To prepare the shanks

Blend the sugar and kosher salt in a bowl and coat the shanks with the mix liberally and thoroughly. Cover and refrigerate overnight.

Preheat oven to 350 degrees.

Before cooking, remove the salt and sugar mix by brushing it off, leaving a light coating. Place the shanks in a roasting pan, cover the bottom of the pan with ½ inch of water, and cover the pan with foil wrap. Bake the shanks, covered, for 90 minutes. Then remove the foil wrap and bake for 15 minutes longer.

Pour the pan juices in a small saucepan and add 1 cup of the apple cider. Reduce by half. This will provide a light jus with which to sauce the shanks. I usually serve some English coarse-grained mustard with the shanks as well.

To make the Poppy Seed Kraut

Core the cabbage and slice it paper thin, creating a slawlike cut. In large saucepan, add the remaining cup of cider, the cider vinegar, salt, and pepper. Bring to a boil and add the cabbage. Toss well and cover with a lid. Simmer the kraut for 10 minutes or until it's tender but not mushy. Add the poppy seeds and toss well. Serve with the shanks. I suggest Killer Rösti Potatoes (see page 63) to complement the dish. And a Côtes du Rhône goes superbly with the pork!

Black Cherry and Chipotle Baby Back Ribs

Makes 4 servings

We all love barbecue, and during our all-too-short Vermont summers we exploit the opportunity to serve our version of ribs. Many have told us that we should bottle our sauce, and I agree—but so much to do and so little time. So here instead is the secret recipe! It's also great on chicken and grilled loin of pork.

INGREDIENTS

4 full racks baby back ribs

¼ cup salt

2 tablespoons pepper

2 tablespoons garlic salt

2 tablespoons chili powder

1 cup minced onions

2 tablespoons minced garlic

24 ounces black cherry preserves

1 can (4–6 ounces) chipotles in adobo, minced

12 ounces tomato paste

1 cup cider vinegar

PREPARATION

Begin by seasoning the ribs with the salt, pepper, garlic salt, and chili powder. Let them sit for 1 hour, refrigerated. Then place them in a roasting pan and cover the bottom with 1 inch of water. Try to keep the ribs standing vertically, if possible, so the spices don't get washed off. Cover tightly with foil wrap and bake in a preheated 300-degree oven for 90 minutes. Set the ribs aside until you're ready to grill.

For the sauce, add enough vegetable oil to a large saucepan to coat the bottom of the pan. Sauté the onions and garlic for 5 minutes over medium heat until they're a medium-brown color. Add all the other ingredients and blend well with a whisk. Reduce the heat to low and simmer for 15 minutes. You may want to thin the sauce a little, and I suggest using some of the braising liquid from the ribs, so don't discard it until you're finished with the sauce.

On a medium-heated charcoal grill, place the ribs on the rack and cook for 4 minutes on each side. Using a pastry brush, begin to liberally paint the sauce on the ribs, cooking for 2 minutes more on each side. You can add more sauce once the ribs are done and on the plates. We like to serve the ribs with Creamy Chipotle Polenta (see page 78) and Tomato Confit (see page 66).

Grilled Yellowfin Tuna with Summer Tomato Cruda

Makes 4 servings

Many people compare yellowfin tuna to beef, and in a lot of ways they are comparable. It's red meat, has the texture of fine beef, and is marbled slightly. The marbling also means that it's important not to overcook the tuna. For the optimal experience, the tuna should be served medium rare. Try to dissuade your guests from demanding a well-done tuna steak. As with all fish, freshness is the key to success: It's paramount that the tuna be of the highest quality, or sushi quality. Look for a vibrant red color with no gray hues at all. The tuna should be firm to the touch with no evidence of separation within the lines of the loin.

I believe that less is more when it comes to serving great tuna. This recipe reflects my goal of showing off the fish by complementing it with just a light sauce and garnish.

PREPARATION

Season both sides of the tuna with the salt and pepper. On a charcoal grill preheated to high, place the tuna steaks at a 45-degree angle and cook for 90 seconds. Rotate the fish

INGREDIENTS

4 tuna steaks, each cut 1 inch thick

1 tablespoon salt

1 teaspoon black pepper

2 cups Tomato Cruda (see page 91)

to the opposite 45-degree angle and cook for 90 seconds more. Turn the fish over and cook for 2 to 3 minutes for medium rare. Remove and serve immediately.

To assemble the plate

Place ½ cup of the Cruda on each plate using a slotted spoon so the juice stays in the container. Place the tuna on top of the Cruda, then spoon the Cruda juice over the top of the fish. I also like to drizzle some balsamic syrup (see page 51) on and around the plate and garnish with a fresh sprig of basil.

A crisp Sauvignon Blanc or Pinot Grigio pairs very well with this dish.

Pan-Roasted Monkfish with Lobster Stock and Barley

Makes 4 servings

Monkfish is sometimes referred to as the poor man's lobster, but I disagree—I think it's better than lobster! The sweet white meat of the monkfish is more tender and versatile than the crustacean and adapts better to various cooking styles.

This recipe shows up on our Mist Grill winter menus as a special and sells out immediately. Several years ago you couldn't give monkfish away; now it rivals in popularity any other fish we feature.

Since the dish doesn't actually use lobsters, making lobster stock without shells is challenging unless you have some in the freezer from a previous recipe. If no stock is available, I suggest using a high-quality seafood, shrimp, or (of course) lobster base or concentrate. All are available from many Internet-based distributors and can be found in better gourmet stores. It's worth stocking your freezer with several varieties—perhaps chicken, beef, lobster, and vegetable bases.

INGREDIENTS

2 quarts lobster stock, divided

6 cups water

2 cups pearl barley

4 monkfish fillets, 6–8 ounces each

2 teaspoons salt

1 teaspoon pepper

2 tablespoons minced shallots

12 threads saffron

2 tablespoons minced fresh tarragon

3 tablespoons butter

16 spinach leaves

PREPARATION

Preheat oven to 350 degrees.

Prepare the lobster stock from scratch if you have the shells available, or prepare the stock according to the instructions on the package of the base or concentrate.

Bring the water and 2 cups of the lobster stock to a boil. Add the barley and cook over low heat, uncovered, for 20 minutes or until the barley is tender to the tooth. Drain off any excess liquid and cool until you're ready to assemble the dish.

Season the fish fillets with the salt and pepper. In a large sauté pan, add enough oil to coat the bottom of the pan. Place it over high heat, add the fillets and shallots, and cook for 3 minutes per side. Bake for 5 minutes. The fish should be firm but still slightly translucent in the center.

To assemble the dish

Bring the remaining stock to a boil and add the saffron and tarragon. Cook for 2 minutes.

Turn off the heat and add the butter, whisking until it's incorporated.

Using large soup bowls, place 4 spinach leaves in the center of each bowl. Slice the monkfish into medallions ½ inch thick. Place the medallions in a shingled circle in the middle of the bowl. Sprinkle ½ cup per portion of the barley around the fish, then ladle 6 ounces of the lobster stock into the bowl. Garnish with a simple sprig of tarragon atop the fish. Serve immediately. The richness of the dish allows it to be paired with a light Pinot Noir or a sturdy, oaky Chardonnay.

Roasted Half Duck with Marinated Apricots and Lingonberry Demiglace

Makes 4 servings

Duck is by far my favorite poultry, with its rustic hint of flavor from the woods and its light gaminess. Duck is considered difficult to prepare by some due to the need to deal with all the fat to get a crisp skin and yet moist meat. Well, this really isn't the case if you take some easy steps in preparation. You'll get great results.

During the fall and winter months we feature duck in various ways, but this recipe is my personal favorite and has appeared on my menus for years.

INGREDIENTS

2 ducks, 3–4 pounds each

1 tablespoon salt

1 teaspoon pepper

1 teaspoon garlic salt

¼ cup hoisin sauce

1 pound dried apricots

1 cup white wine

4 sprigs fresh thyme

3 tablespoons minced shallots

1 pound lingonberries

1 quart veal stock

1 tablespoon minced fresh sage

PREPARATION

To prepare the ducks

Preheat oven to 350 degrees.

Start by splitting the ducks in half and removing the backbone and ribs. Using the tip of a sharp knife, score the skin by cutting through it in ½-inch-wide intervals. Repeat at the opposite angle to get a latticework effect.

Place the half ducks in a roasting pan with a shallow rack and season with the salt, pepper, and garlic salt. Under a broiler, broil the ducks for 8 to 10 minutes, or until most of the fat has rendered out from the cuts in the skin. The shin should be somewhat browned but not blackened at all. Depending on the BTUs of your broiler, you may need to rotate the pan for even and slower rendering. The duck meat should still be raw or just barely cooked at this time, but the skin should be well on its way to doneness.

Drain the fat from the pan, and place the ducks in the roasting pan without the rack. Using a pastry brush, apply an even coating of the hoisin sauce to the skin side of the ducks. Add enough water to the pan to cover the bottom with ¼ inch of water. The water will help steam the undersides of the ducks and add moisture. Bake the ducks for 35 to 40 minutes, or until the skin is crisped and the internal temperature of the duck meat reaches 180 degrees. Remove the ducks from the roasting pan and set aside until you're ready to reheat.

To prepare the apricots

Julienne the apricots into ⅛-inch-thick strips. In a saucepan, combine the apricots, wine, and thyme sprigs and bring to a boil. Turn off the heat and let sit for 15 to 20 minutes. Drain the wine and reserve to use in the sauce. Reserve the apricots for later use as a garnish. Discard the thyme.

To make the sauce

Add enough oil to a saucepan to coat the bottom of the pan, then add the shallots and sauté for 2 minutes, until slightly browned. Add the reserved wine, reduce the heat to medium, and cook for 2 minutes. Add the lingonberries and cook for 2 minutes. Add the veal stock and cook for 15 to 20 minutes or until reduced by about a third. Add the sage and cook for 2 minutes. Season with salt and pepper to taste.

To assemble the dish

Reheat the ducks by placing them in a preheated 350-degree oven for 8 minutes. Then put one duck half on the center of a large plate, ladling ¼ cup of sauce over it. Garnish with 3 to 4 tablespoons of the apricots and serve immediately.

For a great side dish, serve Pan-Mashed Potatoes (see page 65) or Aged Cheddar and Heavy Cream Grits (see page 64). We always suggest a berry-laden Pinot Noir with this dish, as it complements the lingonberries so well.

Jason's Apple Crisp Salmon with Wilted Greens and Reduced Cider

Makes 4 servings

Jason was one of my main men in the kitchen when the Mist Grill opened, and he deserves a ton of credit for the food. Young and talented, he helped create many new dishes that expanded our repertoire. He approached me with an idea for apple crisp salmon and I was very skeptical, but after trying it out I knew he was on to something. A dessert-style crisp topping is a great way to add a crisp outer crust and a sweet caramelized flavor at the same time. The dish was so successful that many diners told us it was the best salmon they'd ever had!

INGREDIENTS

1 quart apple cider

2 cups oats

¼ cup flour

½ cup brown sugar

½ cup butter, melted

2 Granny Smith apples

4 boneless, skinless salmon fillets (6–8 ounces each)

2 teaspoons salt

2 teaspoons pepper

4 cups spinach

4 cups Swiss chard

2 tablespoons butter

PREPARATION

Preheat oven to 350 degrees.

Add the cider to a saucepan and bring it to a boil. Reduce the heat to medium and cook until the cider is reduced by 50 percent. Set aside for later use.

Combine the oats, flour, and brown sugar and mix well. Add the melted butter and blend well by hand.

Cut the apples in half and remove the core and seeds. Slice the apples paper thin.

Season the salmon with equal amounts of the salt and pepper and place in a roasting pan. Cook under the broiler for 6 minutes, or until the fish is lightly browned. Remove from the heat, and place a shingled layer of the apple on top of each fillet. Top with 4 to 5 tablespoons of the crisp topping, evenly coating each fillet with an approximately ¼-inch-thick crust. Bake the fish for 5 minutes.

While the fish is in the oven, add enough oil to a large sauté pan to coat the pan. Over high heat, add the spinach and Swiss chard and quickly wilt the greens. This will only take 60 to 90 seconds. Season with a pinch of salt and pepper.

Bring the reduced cider to a boil, turn off the heat, and whisk in the whole butter.

To assemble the dish

Place an equal amount of the greens in the center of each plate. Place a fillet on top of the pile of greens. Ladle 6 tablespoons of the reduced cider around the plate but not on top of the fish. Serve immediately.

Dijon-Crusted Rack of Lamb

Makes 2 racks (8 chops per rack)

When asked what my favorite dish is, I immediately reply, "Rack of lamb." Hands down, a good rack of lamb and a bottle of good Bordeaux is what God had in mind for the perfect meal. The simplicity of this preparation shows off the naturally great flavor of the lamb—which requires no embellishing. Always an elegant center of the plate at a dinner party, you can serve it unadorned and look like a hero.

INGREDIENTS

2 racks of lamb (8 chops per rack)

2 cups fresh bread crumbs

1 tablespoon minced fresh rosemary

½ cup Dijon mustard

PREPARATION

Preheat oven to 350 degrees.

When you purchase the lamb, ask the butcher to French the bones and to make sure that the chine bone is off. We prefer domestic lamb because the racks are larger, but you can now buy very good, pre-Frenched racks from New Zealand in many stores.

Carefully remove all the fat and silver skin from the bones and the eye of the rack. It's important to have well-trimmed racks with only a little fat left for flavor. The objectionable taste for some comes from the fat of the lamb, not the meat.

Use fresh whole wheat bread for the crumbs, as they adhere better to the mustard and the moisture keeps them fluffy and not too dry. Place the bread in a food processor (if available) and run the machine until the crumbs are uniform but not too fine. You can also do this by hand by chopping with a knife and then crumbling the bread with your hands.

Blend the rosemary into the mustard and coat the meat of the rack fully with a liberal amount of the Dijon mustard mixture. Place the bread crumbs on a plate or tray and roll the mustard-coated portion of the lamb in them. Pat them lightly so the crumbs stick well.

Place the racks in a roasting pan so there's a space under the bones and the racks are curved upward. Bake for 12 to 15 minutes for medium rare. The crumbs should be evenly browned, and the meat should be fairly firm to the touch. Let the racks rest for 3 minutes and then slice between each bone all the way through, creating "lollipops." Arrange 4 chops per plate on or around your side dish of choice.

We often serve Israeli Couscous Risotto-Style (see page 71) and Tomato Confit (see page 66) with this dish. As I said earlier, I love a big red wine with lamb. If you have a fine Bordeaux or a great Cabernet, this is the time to break it out.

Mushroom Tarte Tatin with Parmesan Anglaise and Truffle Oil

Makes 2 servings

Every Mist Grill menu features a vegetarian dish that we try to make interesting. This recipe has become one that we can't take off due to popular demand. It was featured on a PBS TV show, and people have traveled many miles to come try it. It's so good that many nonvegetarians devour it as a regular meal. Playing off the classic French dessert Apple Tarte Tatin, this dish mimics the dessert in its preparation and presentation. It's one of the most "rustified" dishes we serve.

INGREDIENTS

The Sauce

1 cup heavy cream

1 egg yolk

½ cup grated Asiago or Parmesan cheese

salt and pepper to taste

The Tart

1 sheet frozen puff pastry dough

1 tablespoon butter

2 tablespoons minced shallots

1 teaspoon minced garlic

2 cups sliced assorted mushrooms (shiitake, portabella, oyster, chanterelle or any combination of available mushrooms)

1 teaspoon minced fresh herb blend of choice (parsley, sage, rosemary, thyme)

2 pinches salt and 1 pinch pepper

Truffle oil to garnish

PREPARATION

Begin with making the sauce, as this will hold in the refrigerator for 2 or 3 days. Simply reduce the cream by about 40 percent on a low simmer. When it's reduced, remove it from the heat and let cool for 10 minutes. Add the egg yolk and cheese and whisk well, then put it back onto low heat and continue to blend until the sauce just begins to simmer again. Adjust the seasoning with salt and pepper. Remove from the heat and transfer to a clean container.

Preheat oven to 350 degrees.

For the tart, begin by choosing a 7- or 8-inch nonstick sauté pan that can be placed in an oven (no plastic or rubber handle). Using the pan as a template, cut a circle out of the puff pastry sheet. Place the pan onto high heat, add the butter, and let it melt. Add the shallots and garlic and cook for about 30 seconds while stirring. Add the mushrooms and herbs and continue to cook and mix for about 2 minutes. Turn off the heat and place the pastry disk on top of the mushroom mix, sealing the pan. Bake the tart for approxi-mately 8 minutes, or until the pastry has ballooned and turned a rich golden brown.

Carefully remove the pan from the oven and turn the tart out onto a plate, so the pastry crust is on the bottom and the mushrooms are facing up. Immediately return the pan to the stovetop, pour about 4 ounces of the sauce into the pan, and bring to a boil. (This should take about 60 seconds.) Drizzle sauce around the perimeter of the plate and around the tart. Drizzle truffle oil on and around the tart, garnishing with cracked pepper and a fresh herb sprig if desired.

Maple-Glazed Oven-Roasted Chicken with Grilled Apple Hash

Makes 2 servings

Certain aromas that emanate from a kitchen drive people crazy and get their taste buds working overtime. The smell of roasting chicken is one of them; add in the scent of maple syrup caramelizing, and you have a nearly irresistible dish. There is no better maple syrup than that from Vermont, and we're fortunate enough to have several friends who produce some of the state's best. Syrup is graded in the A, B, and C categories, with A being the finest. I actually prefer the B and C grades, which are darker and a bit more rustic in flavor.

PREPARATION

Preheat oven to 350 degrees.

Wash the chicken and remove any innards or gizzards packed in the cavity. Season the skin with the salt, pepper, celery salt, and garlic salt. Place the bird in a shallow roasting pan and bake for 45 minutes. You'll be frequently basting the bird with the maple syrup during this time. Cook the bird for 15 minutes before you begin basting, but then, using a ladle or spoon, drizzle the syrup over the bird a bit at a time until you've used the whole 2 cups. Once all the syrup has been used, continue to baste every 5 minutes with the juices and syrup that have run off into the pan. The bird should be done when the skin is well caramelized and the internal temperature of the leg joint is 180 degrees. Pour all the pan juices into a saucepan and keep simmering over low heat until you're ready to use. Carve the bird into leg, thigh, and breast sections.

INGREDIENTS

1 3-pound roaster chicken

2 teaspoons salt

1 teaspoon pepper

1 teaspoon celery salt

1 teaspoon garlic salt

2 cups maple syrup

4 apples

½ cup paper-thin-shaved onions

1 tablespoon minced fresh sage

¼ cup butter

For the Grilled Apple Hash, grate the apple on a box grater, using the largest-dimension holes, and place in a bowl. Toss the shaved onions with the apples, add the minced sage, and mix.

In a large sauté pan, melt the butter until it just begins to brown. Place 6 tablespoons of the apple mixture in the pan and quickly flatten to the size of a small pancake. You can fit 2 to 4 cakes at once, depending on the size of your pan. Cook for approximately 5 minutes per side, or until browned. The cakes won't stick together very well, so don't fret if they seem to fall apart.

Serve with the chicken immediately, drizzling some of the pan juices and maple sauce over the bird.

Shrimp Churascaritas with Cilantro Chimichurri à la Kirsten

Makes 4 servings

My daughter Kirsten's favorite dish is this one. She'll eat almost anything, which I think is great for teens in today's world, but she'd choose this over a bowl of ice cream anytime! *Churascaritas* is a name I made up for a line of menu items served by a restaurant chain based in Dallas, Texas. They had been searching for an alternative to fajitas, so I developed a hybrid of a Brazilian and Argentinean style of preparing meats called churascaria with fajita and came up with churascaritas! Really quite simple, the meats or shrimp are skewered and highly seasoned then grilled on open flames. During the summer we cook hundreds of these shrimp delicacies every week.

Chimichurri is a Latin condiment that's a cross between pesto and vinaigrette. Most are traditionally made with parsley, but I love the fresh tang from cilantro in this dish.

INGREDIENTS

2 tablespoons salt

1 teaspoon pepper

1 teaspoon garlic salt

2 tablespoons chili powder

2 tablespoons cumin powder

20 shrimp (10–12 count per pound)

1 cup minced fresh cilantro (pack the cup full)

¼ cup minced garlic

1 jalapeño pepper, minced, with seeds

1 cup fresh lime juice

¼ cup orange juice

½ cup olive oil

PREPARATION

Blend the salt with the pepper, garlic salt, chili powder, and cumin. Set aside until you're ready to use it.

Peel and devein the shrimp, leaving the tails on. Carefully split the shrimp almost all the way through and open up each one so it looks like a butterfly. Lay 5 of the shrimp in a line with the tails alternating from left to right. The shrimp should be flat and the butterfly wings spread out. Using wooden skewers, carefully skewer the shrimp with one skewer running up the left side and one running up the right side. If done properly, the two skewers will keep the shrimp flat and spread the meat apart. The skewers should be parallel to each other the width of the shrimp lengths.

Evenly sprinkle the seasoning blend on both sides of the shrimp. Refrigerate for 30 minutes to let the spices adhere well to the shrimp.

To make the chimichurri

In a mixing bowl, add the cilantro, garlic, jalapeño, lime juice, orange juice, and olive oil. Blend well. Let this mixture sit at room temperature for 30 minutes.

To assemble the dish

Preheat the charcoal grill to its highest temperature. Place the shrimp on the grill and cook for 2 minutes on each side or until they're slightly firm to the touch. Serve immediately over plain white rice, or Grilled Chipotle Polenta Cakes (see page 78), with chimichurri spooned atop. Fresh-sliced lime and a sprig of cilantro makes a fine garnish.

Stevie's Alfredo Carbonara

Makes 4 to 6 servings

My son is a true foodie, as he has grown up in the restaurant business his whole life. Like his sister, he'll eat almost anything he's served, but he could be very happy eating carbonara every day of his life. I must admit I could too! This hearty pasta dish may be the ultimate country variation of carbonara as well as the richest recipe in the entire cookbook—as you'll see from the ingredients.

INGREDIENTS

1 pound spaghetti

8 ounces smoked bacon, diced

¼ cup diced onions

1 tablespoon minced garlic

1 tablespoon crushed red pepper flakes

6 egg yolks

1 quart heavy cream, divided

1½ cups grated Parmesan cheese

1 cup frozen peas

PREPARATION

Cook the pasta per normal instructions; drain and rinse with cold water. Set aside until you're ready to use it. Be sure to cook the pasta al dente.

In a 12- to 14-inch sauté pan, add the bacon and cook until the fat is rendered and it's slightly browned. Add the onions and garlic and cook for 3 minutes while stirring. Add the crushed red pepper flakes and reduce the heat to low.

In a small bowl, whisk the egg yolks with 1 cup of the cream. Set aside.

Add the remaining 3 cups of cream to the sauté pan and simmer for 10 minutes. Add the egg mixture and Parmesan and blend well. Cook for 2 minutes or until the cheese is melted and the sauce is smooth. Add the peas and cook for 1 minute

Add the pasta to the sauté pan and, using a pair of tongs, toss to evenly coat the pasta and heat it. Serve immediately.

This rich pasta deserves a solid Chianti Riserva to cut through the richness and the smoky bacon. Bon appetito!

Chicken Saltimboca "Sinatra"

Makes 4 servings

The Sinatra song "My Way" reflects our approach to many of the dishes we re-create from old traditional recipes. This saltimboca plays to the old classic but reflects some Mist Grill touches. Prosciutto adds a great saltiness and silky texture, and the Fontina cheese tops it all with a creamy and nutty flavor.

INGREDIENTS

4 boneless, skinless chicken breasts

2 tablespoons minced shallots

2 tablespoons minced garlic

¼ cup sherry

¼ cup lemon juice

1 cup chicken stock

1 tablespoon minced fresh sage

1 tablespoon grated lemon zest

½ teaspoon black pepper

4 thin slices Fontina cheese

8 thin slices prosciutto

2 tablespoons butter

PREPARATION

Preheat oven to 375 degrees.

Trim the chicken breasts of any excess fat and pound them with a mallet so they're slightly flattened. Add enough olive oil to a large sauté pan to coat the pan well. Place the pan on high heat, add the chicken, and cook for 3 minutes on each side or until medium brown in color. Remove the chicken breasts and place them on a baking pan. Immediately add the shallots and garlic to the sauté pan and sauté for 1 minute (you may need to add a little more oil). Add the sherry to deglaze the pan, and then add the lemon juice and chicken stock. Cook for 2 minutes, then add the sage, lemon zest, and black pepper. Reduce the heat to a simmer.

Place a slice of the Fontina on each breast and two slices of the prosciutto on top of the Fontina. Bake for 5 minutes.

Add the butter to the sauce and blend well. Serve the chicken with the sauce poured over the breasts.

I suggest serving this dish with Risotto Cakes (see page 67) and Grilled Ratatouille (see page 70). A Chianti or Barolo pairs well with this, as does a monster Chardonnay!

Summer Vegetable and Portabella Napoleon

Makes 4 servings

This simple compilation of vegetables always has diners saying *wow!* Basic preparation lets the natural flavors shine through, and the presentation is easy and attractive. As with the Mushroom Tarte Tatin (see page 102), this started out as a vegetarian dish but was so well received that it has become a mainstay of regular menu offerings for the nonveggie crowd as well.

INGREDIENTS

8 large portabella mushroom caps

1 zucchini

1 yellow squash

1 red onion

4 red peppers

salt and pepper to taste

8 ounces goat cheese

24 spinach leaves

1 cup Balsamic Vinaigrette (see page 151)

Mesclun mix for serving

PREPARATION

Remove the stems of the mushrooms and scoop out the gills with a spoon. Slice the zucchini and yellow squash into planks ¼ inch thick. Slice the onion into ¼-inch-thick disks; try to keep them from becoming onion rings. Roast the peppers (see the instructions on page 30), peel them, and cut the fillets into ½-inch-wide strips. Lightly oil the portabellas, onions, zucchini, and squash. Season with salt and pepper. On a charcoal grill, grill the vegetables until they're lightly browned on both sides. The onions will take longer than the rest; they should be tender.

On an oiled baking sheet, place one of the portabellas with the top side down. Place a slice of the onion on the mushroom, and then a thin layer of the goat cheese. Repeat this process with each of the vegetables and spinach leaves and then place another mushroom top-side up to cap it off (pun intended). The result should be layered vegetables with a thin layer of goat cheese between each one. You can prepare these a day ahead; reheat in a 350-degree oven for 10 minutes. Serve with some mesclun mix and a drizzle of the Balsamic Vinaigrette over the dish.

Shrimp Tarte Tatin with Roasted Tomatoes and Calamata Olives

Makes 1 tart

Given the success of the Mushroom Tarte Tatin (see page 102) I had to expand the line with some other versions. This shrimp variation is great; the finished dish is similar to an upside-down potpie with an attitude. As with the mushroom version, I suggest using the frozen puff pastry and having the ingredients prepped ahead of time so you can cook the dish to order.

INGREDIENTS

7 shrimp (16–20 count per pound)

1 puff pastry sheet

2 plum tomatoes

salt and pepper to taste

2 tablespoons diced green peppers

2 tablespoons pitted and chopped Calamata olives

1 tablespoon minced garlic cloves

1 tablespoon minced fresh basil

½ teaspoon minced fresh rosemary

PREPARATION

Preheat oven to 375 degrees.

Peel and devein the shrimp and remove the tails. Keep refrigerated until you're ready to use them.

Cut the puff pastry into a 6-inch circle; it helps to use the pan you'll be working with as the template. Keep the pastry refrigerated until use.

Cut the tomatoes in half lengthwise and place them cut-side up on an oiled baking sheet. Season with a pinch of salt and pepper and roast them for 20 minutes or until they're browned on the edges.

In a 6-inch ovenproof sauté pan, add enough oil to coat the pan. Add the green peppers, olives, and garlic and sauté for 2 minutes. Remove the pan from the heat. Place the tomatoes in the pan skin-side down; put one each at 12, 3, 6, and 9 o'clock. Place the shrimp between the tomatoes and sprinkle the herbs over all the ingredients. Place the 6-inch-round disk of puff pastry on top of the ingredients and press it down to conform to the inside of the pan. Bake for 10 to 12 minutes, or until the pastry is puffed up and evenly browned to a medium shade.

Carefully flip the tart onto a large plate and serve immediately. The presentation should have the pastry on the bottom as the crust; the ingredients should be symmetrical on top.

Grilled Veal Chop with Wild Mushroom Ragout and Truffled Demiglace

Makes 4 servings

If I had to make a choice for a "last meal," it'd be a toss-up between rack of lamb and a veal chop. Knowing who was cooking might make a difference, but it would still be a tough call.

There's nothing more delicate than a great veal chop. The tender meat with its subtly sweet natural flavor lends itself well to a number of recipes, but combined with the earthy flavor of mushrooms and the sensuous aroma and taste of truffles—well, this is one of the Mist Grill's killer plates.

PREPARATION

In a medium saucepan, add enough oil to coat the pan. Sauté the shallots for 2 minutes and add the red wine. Cook for 1 minute and add the veal stock. Reduce the heat to low and simmer for 15 minutes, then remove the pan from the heat.

Preheat a charcoal grill to high. Season the veal chops on both sides with salt and pepper. Place the chops on the grill at 45-degree angles and cook for 3 minutes; rotate to the opposite 45-degree angle and cook for 3 minutes longer. Turn the chops over and cook for 6 minutes. Reduce the temperature to medium, or move the chops to the cooler edges of the grill. The veal should be served with a light pink center or just below medium doneness. To check for doneness, use the pressure test: The veal should be slightly firm when pressed on. Depending on the temper-

INGREDIENTS

2 tablespoons minced shallots

¼ cup red wine

2 cups veal stock

4 veal chops, 10–12 ounces each

salt and pepper to taste

2 tablespoons butter

2 cups Mushroom Ragout (see Wild Mushroom and Goat Cheese Tartlets on page 52)

4 teaspoons white truffle oil

ature of your grill, you may need to cook for 3 or 4 minutes longer. Remember, it's better to be underdone than overdone! You can always cook a little more if needed.

To assemble the dish

Heat the sauce to a simmer, add the butter, and whisk until it's incorporated. Heat the Mushroom Ragout. Place a veal chop in the center of each plate and spoon an equal amount of the ragout on top of each chop. Ladle approximately 5 tablespoons of the sauce over and around the chop. Drizzle a teaspoon of the truffle oil on top of the ragout and serve immediately. This dish cries out for a great Burgundy, Pinot Noir, or Syrah. Enjoy!

SWEET REWARDS

When I was growing up, my parents ensured that my siblings and I cleaned our plates by using a reliable and time-honored threat: Finish your dinner or *no dessert.* (Although the real question, considering the robust appetites of the large-sized Schimoler kids, was whether each of us would get enough of the main course.) However, knowing the odds were good that we would all "deserve" dessert, my mother never seemed to forget it.

I grew up in the countryside of Long Island with a productive apple orchard. There was also one unproductive pear tree and some cherry trees. The birds somehow knew exactly when to descend on the cherries—inevitably, the day before we'd decided to pick. But the apple trees were quite the opposite. We had several varieties growing: Baldwins, Cortlands, and a hybrid Macintosh-Cortland. All the trees were well cared for, and they produced tons of apples of an amazingly high quality over the years.

My mother embraced the challenge of creating new apple recipes from this cornucopia: apple pie, apple crisp, apple cobbler, baked apples, fritters, pancakes, smooth applesauce, chunky applesauce, apple side dishes, and home-pressed apple cider. Needless to say, the desserts she served inevitably had apples in the mix, but we never objected; my mother's apple pie really is the best I've ever eaten. Most of all, we loved the idea that the apples we grew, cared for, picked, and peeled were so good! Most of the desserts from those days would be called comfort foods today, and the desserts we bake at the Mist Grill reflect such simple goodness. Pies, cobblers, crisps, fools, grunts, and tarts can always be found on our dessert menu, and the fresh tastes and textures are hard to improve on. Simply adding some fresh whipped cream, a dollop of crème fraîche, or a pool of crème anglaise is all we do to enhance our country-style desserts. We do offer desserts that are a little more innovative and sometimes a bit wacky, but it's the simple rustic desserts that people enjoy most.

When customers enter the Mist Grill, they walk right into our bakery area and are immediately surrounded by the smells of freshly baked bread, cookies, and pies. Aromas can trigger strong memories of past experiences, and the aromas of such familiar desserts as apple pie laced with cinnamon and nutmeg, or meltingly fragrant chocolate chip cookies, return some people to childhood visits to Grandmother's house. Better times, family, friends, celebration, anticipation, and, yes, the sweet reward following the feast!

The recipes in this chapter try to evoke a time when dessert was a reward for finishing dinner. Not that we insist on it at the Mist Grill, but I do walk around the dining room from time to time, inspecting customers' plates and letting them know that if they've cleaned their plates, they've earned dessert! Even though I do it in jest, our guests do indeed look forward to a warm slice of apple pie served with a bit of aged Vermont Cheddar and a cup of hand-roasted coffee to close out the evening.

When you're serving dessert at home after a casual family dinner or following a special dinner party, you're bringing the evening together in a relaxing way, and presenting a memorable last impression for your guests to savor. And perhaps with your own special apple pie recipe, you're creating a sense memory for someone else who will remember this meal for years to come. Enjoy the rewards!

Vermont Maple Crème Brûlée

Makes 6 to 8 servings

This is by far the most popular dessert at the Mist Grill. I have traveled extensively and will order crème brûlée wherever I go, to test the various versions. It's hard to improve on the classic version when prepared well, but our addition of maple syrup makes it very Vermont and adds a sweet element that's hard to beat.

INGREDIENTS

½ cup sugar

1 cup egg yolks

3 cups heavy cream

¼ cup maple syrup

2 teaspoons vanilla extract

1 teaspoon maple extract

⅓ cup granulated brown sugar

PREPARATION

Preheat oven to 350 degrees.

In a mixing bowl, combine the sugar and egg yolks and mix well with a whisk. Add all the other ingredients and whisk until they're fully blended. Pour the cream mixture into 4- to 6-ounce ramekins, filling to 90 percent capacity. Place them in a shallow roasting pan and add warm water until the water comes halfway up the sides of the ramekins. Bake for 35 to 45 minutes or until the centers are set. Remove from the water bath and chill. Remove from the refrigerator 30 minutes before serving.

To caramelize the sugar on top, sprinkle brown sugar evenly across the surface of the custards. The layer should be thin. Under a heated broiler, place the custards as close as possible to the heating element and melt until the sugar is browned; this will take 60 to 90 seconds. At the restaurant we use a small propane torch from the hardware store and simply apply the direct heat from the flame to caramelize the sugar. This takes only a few seconds and doesn't risk cooking the custard, the way you can if you leave it under a broiler too long. If you are using a broiler, be sure to watch the process carefully: The sugar will transform from nicely caramelized to burned in a matter of seconds.

Pear and Ginger Tarte Tatin with Allspice Anglaise

Makes one 6-serving tarte

The first time I had Tarte Tatin I fell in love: It was a dessert that I could eat for breakfast every day. The classic version is made with apples, but I substituted pears one evening when I realized that we'd run out of apples. Then I played around a bit more, and the finished results were outstanding! The pears worked great as a stand-in for the apples, the gingerroot I added provided a fresh spiciness to the fruit, and the allspice I put into the cream sauce imparted a peppery flavor that was wonderful.

I continue to make it this way; I haven't picked up an apple to make Tarte Tatin in more than three years.

INGREDIENTS

The Tarte

7 pears

1½ cups sugar

¼ cup water

2 tablespoons grated fresh gingerroot

1 teaspoon cinnamon

2 10-inch piecrusts

The Allspice Anglaise

2 cups whole milk

1 vanilla bean, split lengthwise

½ cup sugar

6 large to extra-large egg yolks

1 teaspoon ground allspice or white pepper

PREPARATION

To make the tart

Preheat oven to 350 degrees.

Peel and halve the pears. Slice them lengthwise starting just below the stem area; keep the top portion intact. Try to get 4 or 5 slices per pear. This will create a fan effect.

In a 10-inch nonstick sauté pan, add the sugar and water and over medium heat, stirring to dissolve the sugar. Continue to heat while the sugar transforms from a liquid to a crystal and back to a liquid again. When the sugar turns from crystal back into liquid, it will be a very light amber and will continue to caramelize very quickly; cook it too long and the sugar will burn. Sugar at this temperature is very hot. Do not touch it at all—it will provide a burn that you'll remember!

As soon as the sugar is light brown, remove the pan from the heat and carefully place the pears in the pan with the rounded side facing down. Configure the pears so the stem side is pointing to the middle of the pan. You should get 6 pears on the perimeter; place the final pear in the center. Evenly sprinkle the ginger and the cinnamon over the pears. Place both of the piecrusts on top, lightly press down the dough, and crimp the edges up against the side of the pan to seal the tart. The double crust will ensure a sturdy bottom when the tart is inverted. Bake for 20 minutes or until the crust is golden brown.

Let the pan cool for 15 minutes, then place a serving tray or large plate over it. Carefully and quickly turn the pan over and let the tart fall out onto the plate. This is always a rewarding event! The tart will hold for a full day but is best when devoured shortly after it's baked.

To make the allspice anglaise

Put the milk in a saucepan and add the vanilla bean. Over low heat, begin to bring the milk to a simmer. While the milk is coming up to temperature, whisk together the sugar, egg yolks, and allspice in a mixing bowl.

When the milk comes to a simmer, remove the bean. Scrape out any remaining seeds and add them back to the milk. Slowly pour half the milk into the egg mixture while whisking. When you're done, put the mixture back into the pan and continue to cook over low heat. Do not bring this to a boil! Cook until the sauce coats the back of a spoon without fully dripping off. Be sure to stir constantly; don't forget the edges of the pan, where the sauce will curdle if it's not stirred. Remove from the heat and continue to stir for 2 minutes.

Strain the sauce through a mesh strainer into a bowl and refrigerate immediately. Let it cool for at least 2 hours, stirring occasionally to help it cool more evenly and to prevent a skin from forming. Serve chilled with the warm tarte.

Gingerbread Bomb

Makes 6 servings

This is one of those recipes that came about from desperation. We had run out of all our desserts at the end of a very busy weekend, and as usual during Sunday Suppers we were making things up at the last second. I had a pan of overbaked gingerbread that was too dry to serve. So I quickly rummaged through the refrigerator and emerged with a quart of pastry cream, some chocolate sauce, and some whipped cream.

The ginger cake needed moisture, so I cut a hole in the middle of a square slice of the cake, removed the "plug," and filled the hole with pastry cream. Then I covered the hole with some of the plug, hiding the pastry cream. I coated the whole thing with the chocolate sauce and topped it off with a dollop of the whipped cream. I immediately brought three of the "bombs" to a table of diners who were waiting for dessert, saying, "I don't know if you'll like these, so they're on the house." After they finished, they insisted on paying for the Gingerbread Bombs—which have been on the menu ever since!

PREPARATION

To make the gingerbread cake

Preheat oven to 350 degrees.

Cream the butter until it's light in color. Add the sugar and molasses and blend well. Add the egg and beat until the mixture is fluffy.

Blend all the dry ingredients together in a separate mixing bowl. Add the dry ingredients to the butter mixture alternately with the

INGREDIENTS

The Gingerbread Cake

6 tablespoons butter

1 cup brown sugar

½ cup molasses

1 egg

2½ cups all-purpose flour

1 teaspoon baking soda

1 teaspoon ginger powder

1 teaspoon cinnamon

½ teaspoon salt

¾ cup buttermilk

The Pastry Cream

1 cup milk

2 tablespoons unsalted butter

4 large egg yolks

¼ cup sugar

3 tablespoons all-purpose flour

¼ teaspoon salt

1 tablespoon vanilla extract

The Chocolate Sauce

2 ounces semisweet baking chocolate

¼ cup unsalted butter

½ cup hot water (100–120 degrees)

⅔ cup packed brown sugar

2 teaspoons vanilla extract

buttermilk until fully blended.

Pour the mixture into a greased 9- or 10-inch cake pan. Bake for 40 to 45 minutes.

To make the pastry cream

Heat the milk and butter in a saucepan until simmering. Combine the egg yolks, sugar, flour, and salt in a mixing bowl. Drizzle the hot liquid into the egg mixture slowly while whisking. When it's fully incorporated, pour the mixture back in the saucepan and bring to a boil while stirring constantly. Remove from the heat and add the vanilla, continuing to stir for 60 seconds to help the mixture cool. Pour into a bowl and cover the surface with plastic wrap. Refrigerate for at least 2 hours. Stir the cream prior to using.

To make the chocolate sauce

In a double boiler, melt the chocolate and butter. Blend in the water and whisk until it's fully blended. Add the sugar and vanilla, blend well, and continue to cook for 4 to 5 minutes.

To assemble the dessert

Using a 3-inch-wide cookie or pastry cutter, cut out a round disk from the cake. Using an apple corer, core the center of the cake disk, reserving the plug of cake. Fill the center hole three-quarters full with pastry cream. Insert a piece of the core to fill the hole; it should extend from the top of the cake about ½ inch. Place the cake on a plate and drizzle with the warm chocolate sauce to enrobe it. Garnish with a dollop of fresh whipped cream. Serve immediately.

Chocolate Almond Torte

Makes 8 to 10 servings

This recipe comes from Nancy Silverton of Campanile and La Brea Breads in California. Nancy is one of our Chef Stuff Chefs and has long been an inspiration for bakers. This cake was featured in several of our menus for Neiman Marcus and Macy's by Mail; we serve it at the Mist Grill as well. It's been changed a bit, but it provides a wonderfully sinful cake that will require only a thin slice to get the job done.

PREPARATION

To make the torte

Preheat oven to 350 degrees.

In a mixing bowl, cream the butter until it's softened. Add the sugar and mix until light and fluffy. Add the almond paste bit by bit and mix well. Add the cocoa powder and blend until fully incorporated. Add the eggs one at a time, blending well. Pour the batter into a greased 9-inch springform pan and bake for 20 to 25 minutes or until the cake is slightly firm to the touch in the center. Let it cool, then apply the glaze.

INGREDIENTS

The Torte

1 cup unsalted butter

1 cup sugar

1 cup almond paste

¾ cup cocoa powder

5 extra-large eggs

The Glaze

1 pound semisweet chocolate, chopped

¼ cup light corn syrup

¾ pound unsalted butter

To make the glaze

Combine the chocolate, corn syrup, and butter in a stainless-steel mixing bowl. In a double boiler over simmering water, melt the ingredients while stirring until smooth. Let the mix cool for 3 to 4 minutes, then pour over the cake and, with a spatula, evenly spread it over the cake's top and down its sides. Let the glaze set up for 10 to 15 minutes before serving. Garnish the top of the cake with sliced, toasted almonds if you desire.

Lemon Curd Sandwich with Berry Sauce

Makes 4 to 6 servings

This dessert is a wonderful, light finish to a meal—and it pairs so well with a sweet Muscat dessert wine, it's as if they were made for each other. The tangy and sweet lemon curd layered between crisp wafers of phyllo with a drizzle of fresh berry sauce tastes great, and the presentation is unpretentious yet simply elegant. The recipe for the lemon curd is a bit nontraditional: I fold in fresh whipped cream at the last minute, making it more airy.

PREPARATION

To make the lemon curd

In a nonreactive saucepan, combine the lemon juice, zest, sugar, butter, and water over low heat and cook, stirring, until the butter is melted. Combine all the eggs and egg yolks and whisk well. Slowly add a quarter of the butter mixture to the eggs while continuing to whisk, then add the mixture back to the saucepan and continue to cook over low heat, stirring, until the mixture becomes thick. This should take 3 to 4 minutes. Transfer to a bowl, cover the surface with plastic wrap, and refrigerate for at least 3 hours, or until well chilled.

To make the phyllo crisps

Preheat oven to 350 degrees.

Carefully peel off one sheet of the phyllo dough at a time and lay it flat on a clean table surface or cutting board. Quickly cover the entire sheet with a thin coat of the melted butter. Sprinkle a small amount of the sugar evenly across the sheet. Place another sheet of

INGREDIENTS

The Lemon Curd

½ cup fresh lemon juice

zest from 1 large lemon

½ cup sugar

½ cup unsalted butter

2 teaspoons water

3 large eggs

4 large egg yolks

1 cup heavy cream

The Phyllo Crisps

1 box phyllo dough

½ cup melted unsalted butter

½ cup sugar

The Berry Sauce

1 pint fresh raspberries

1 pint fresh blackberries

2 cups water

¼ cup sugar

the dough on top of the first, again coating it with melted butter and a sprinkle of sugar. Place a third sheet on top, but keep it plain. Cut the sheet into six equal pieces; this should yield approximately six 3-by-3-inch squares.

Repeat the phyllo laminating process for as many squares as you'll need. You'll use three squares for each dessert.

Place the squares on a lightly greased baking

continued next page

sheet or a piece of parchment paper; place another baking sheet on top of the squares so that it nests inside the first pan and weighs the squares down to keep them from curling. Bake for 10 minutes or until just golden brown. Place the squares on a clean pan until you're ready to use them.

To make the berry sauce

Combine all ingredients in a saucepan and bring to a boil. Reduce the heat and simmer for 15 minutes. Let the mixture cool for 10 to 15 minutes, then place it in a blender. Blend until smooth, then strain through a mesh strainer to remove the seeds. Refrigerate for 1 hour prior to serving.

To assemble the dessert

Whip the cream and fold this into the lemon curd. Place one of the squares in the center of a plate. Spoon approximately 2 tablespoons of the lemon curd onto the square. Place another square atop the curd. Spoon on another 2 tablespoons of curd, then place the third square on top. Drizzle the berry sauce around the plate. Garnish with a fresh sprig of mint and a light dusting of powdered sugar if desired.

Apple and Bourbon Bread Pudding

Makes 4 to 6 servings

There may be no dessert more rustic than bread pudding. The use of crusty bread of any type, rich custard, and anything else you have hanging around the kitchen inevitably produces a soul-warming dessert loved by everyone. The apples give this recipe some extra moisture and flavor; with the addition of a bit of bourbon, the bread pudding starts to become something more than just bread pudding.

We generally give this dessert a very simple presentation: a dollop of fresh whipped cream is all a classic dish such as this needs.

INGREDIENTS

½ cup raisins

½ cup bourbon

4 medium apples, peeled and diced

2 cups milk

1 cup sugar

3 extra-large eggs

1 tablespoon vanilla extract

¼ teaspoon cinnamon

¼ teaspoon nutmeg

4 cups stale bread (preferably French), cut in ½-inch cubes

2 tablespoons butter

PREPARATION

Soak the raisins in the bourbon overnight.

Preheat the oven to 350 degrees.

In a large mixing bowl, combine all the ingredients except the raisin mixture and the bread and butter and whisk well to blend. Pour the milk mixture over the bread cubes and toss well. Add the raisins and bourbon, and mix by folding the ingredients. Let this soak for 30 minutes, gently mixing several times.

Melt the butter in a shallow baking pan (1-quart capacity), letting it coat the bottom of the pan. Pour the bread mixture into the pan and bake for 35 to 40 minutes or until the custard is set and a knife comes out clean when inserted. Let the pudding cool for at least 15 minutes. Serve warm with fresh whipped cream. You can also pour a splash of bourbon on the dessert just prior to serving.

Peach and Basil Ice Cream

Makes 4 servings

Being located in the same town as Ben and Jerry's puts some pressure on anyone who tries to sell ice cream. We take a different approach. Yes, you will find various Ben and Jerry's flavors in our freezer, but we love to make interesting combinations of our own as well. Ice cream can be very easy to make at home, but it does require some type of ice cream machine. Whether this is a fancy electric model or an old-fashioned hand-crank system that uses ice and salt, there's great reward and satisfaction when you scoop out that first taste of your own concoction. This recipe uses a very basic custard mix that can be the foundation for an endless combination of flavors.

The peach and basil combination may sound a bit out there, but it screams *summer*—and the sweet natural anise flavor from the basil adds a whole new dimension of flavor to the peaches and custard. Served as is or as a topping for a crisp, cobbler, or pie, your guests will want more of this delicious combination. Note that this recipe doesn't call for eggs or for any cooking, making it quick and easy.

INGREDIENTS

4 fresh ripe peaches, peeled, pitted, and diced

⅓ cup sugar

¼ cup minced fresh basil

2 teaspoons vanilla extract

2 cups half-and-half

PREPARATION

Combine the peaches, sugar, basil, and vanilla in a mixing bowl. Using a wooden spoon, mix well, slightly mashing the peaches. Let the mix sit for 30 minutes. Add the half-and-half and stir. Pour the mix into your ice cream machine and follow the manufacturer's instructions to freeze the mix. Place in the freezer until fully frozen, removing several minutes before serving to let the ice cream soften slightly. Feel free to experiment with the ingredients, adding more basil if you're looking for a little more of a hit of anise flavor.

For your more conservative guests, simply don't tell them that there's basil in the ice cream. I guarantee they'll be wondering what the secret ingredient is that makes this dessert so wonderful and interesting!

Summary Fruit Strudel

Makes 8 slices

With my German heritage, I must have a genetic propensity to like strudel! As a child I ate tons of strudel, and mostly for breakfast. I still eat a slice almost every morning with some of Mané's hand-roasted coffee, and I don't plan on changing the habit anytime soon. We use fruits of the season, and my favorite time is when the summer fruits are at the market.

3 fresh peaches, peeled, pitted, and sliced

½ pint sliced fresh strawberries

½ pint fresh raspberries

½ pint fresh blackberries

¼ cup sugar

2 tablespoons fresh-grated gingerroot

1½ teaspoons vanilla extract

¼ cup cornstarch

1 sheet frozen puff pastry dough

1 egg

2 tablespoons water

2 tablespoons sugar in the raw

PREPARATION

Combine all the fruit with the sugar, gingerroot, and vanilla in a large bowl and toss well. Sift in the cornstarch a bit at a time and toss well to coat evenly. Set aside.

Lay the puff pastry sheet on a lightly floured surface and, using a rolling pin, roll the sheet to gain approximately 2 inches in each direction. Place the fruit in the center of the sheet and mound it up so it's approximately 10 inches long, 3 inches wide, and 2 inches high. You may have a little extra fruit, but don't overstuff the center. Using a sharp knife, cut the long sides of the sheet by cutting 2-inch-wide strips inward 2 inches. The result should look like ribbons attached to the sheet and ending approximately 1 inch from the fruit.

Fold the wide ends of the sheet up around the fruit; the dough should cover at least 1 inch of the fruit. Then take each ribbon and gently stretch it up and over the fruit so it reaches about halfway over. Take the opposite-side ribbon and stretch it over the first. Continue to wrap the strudel with the ribbons from one end to the other. When it's fin-ished, the strudel should be crimped tightly at the ends to prevent leaking; adjust the ribbons if necessary to completely cover the fruit. You can gently adjust the shape of the entire strudel to make it more uniform. The final strudel should be 10 to 11 inches long by 4 to 5 inches wide.

Preheat the oven to 350 degrees. Whisk the egg with the water and paint the entire strudel with the egg wash. This will help "glue" the strudel, as well as providing some glossy browning. Sprinkle the sugar in the raw evenly over the strudel and bake on a jelly roll pan for 25 to 30 minutes or until it's deep golden brown and some of the fruit begins to bubble through the ribbons. Let the strudel cool for 15 to 20 minutes and serve.

Open Apple Croustade with Cinnamon Cream

Makes 4 croustades

These free-form croustades taste much like apple pie—and they actually are mini apple pies without the pie tin. With the edges of the crust folded roughly over the apples, these look like the apple tarts of 200 years ago.

If you haven't already noticed it, I'm a sucker for the homey smell and taste of fresh apple pie. This simple version lives up to all expectations.

If you want to buy prepared refrigerated piecrust to make life easy, I won't tell.

INGREDIENTS

2 10-inch piecrusts

4 apples, peeled, cored, and cut in ¼-inch slices

¼ teaspoon nutmeg

½ teaspoon ginger powder

2 tablespoons brown sugar

3 tablespoons currants

1½ teaspoons vanilla extract, divided

1 cup heavy cream

¼ teaspoon cinnamon

PREPARATION

Preheat oven to 350 degrees.

Begin by rolling out the piecrusts on a lightly floured surface to increase the size of the dough by 2 inches all around. Use a 5-inch plate or circle as a template and cut two circles from each piece of dough. Place them in the refrigerator until you're ready to use them.

In a large bowl, combine the apples with the nutmeg, ginger, brown sugar, currants, and 1 teaspoon of the vanilla. Toss well to coat evenly. Place a dough disk on a baking sheet and put approximately one-quarter of the apple mixture in the center. Begin to fold the dough in pleats toward the center of the apples. Continue until you've completed the circle of pleated folds, leaving the top center open approximately 1 inch. The croustade should look like a small volcano. Repeat with all the dough disks.

Bake for 15 to 18 minutes or until the crust is golden brown. Whip the cream until it's just stiff and whisk in the cinnamon and remaining ½ teaspoon vanilla. Serve the croustades warm with whipped cream dolloped on top.

Apple Crisp Pie with Sharp Cheddar

Makes one 9-inch pie

This simple pie is served at all meals at the Mist Grill—including breakfast!

It's truly a Yankee tradition to serve apple pie with Cheddar cheese. The early Vermonters were definitely on to something when that first slice of tangy old Cheddar made its way onto a hot piece of apple pie. The combination for some seems less than appealing, but all it takes is one taste of some classic extra-sharp Vermont Cheddar, the sweet crisp bite of fresh apples, and a buttery piecrust for you to forget the ice cream and grab the Cheddar!

INGREDIENTS

1½ cups oats

¼ cup flour

½ cup brown sugar

½ cup butter, melted

1 10-inch piecrust

1½ recipes Open Apple Croustade filling
 (see page 128)

8 ounces extra-sharp Vermont Cheddar
 cheese

PREPARATION

Preheat oven to 350 degrees.

Combine the oats, brown sugar, flour, and melted butter in a large bowl to make the crisp topping. In a 9-inch pie tin or pie plate, form the crust to the tin and create a crust edge by crimping the edges to flute or using the tines of a fork. Fill the pie with the apple filling, then evenly cover the apples with the crisp topping. Be sure to coat evenly with ½ inch of the crisp topping. Gently tamp the crisp topping down and fill in any holes.

Bake on a cookie sheet for 25 to 30 minutes or until the edge of the crust is deep golden brown. Let the pie cool for 30 to 60 minutes to let it set up. Slice the cheese paper thin and cover each slice of pie with 2 to 3 slices of it. Warm in the oven for 4 to 5 minutes or until the cheese just starts to melt. Serve immediately.

Apple Cider and Dried Cranberry Granita

Makes 8 servings

Granitas are easy to make from a technical perspective—you really don't need any fancy tools or machines—but the results are so rewarding when you scoop out that first spoon of the colorful and interesting combination of flavors. Granita is a crude form of frozen water, sugar, and flavors that looks like cut glass or shiny quartz. We love to serve an interesting granita during the summer months as a refreshing light dessert, but we more often serve them as palate cleansers during a tasting menu at a wine dinner, between the seafood course and another appetizer or big plate.

There are no limits to the flavors or ingredients you can add to a granita, so after you've been through the process once, feel free to play around and experiment with your own favorite concoctions. One key thing to remember, however, is that the sugar and alcohol content helps keep the ice from becoming totally frozen; this will keep your granita soft.

INGREDIENTS

4 cups apple cider

¼ cup sugar

½ cup dried cranberries

¼ cup brandy or apple brandy

2 tablespoons lemon juice

PREPARATION

Combine all ingredients in a bowl and mix well to dissolve the sugar. Pour the mixture into a clean shallow metal pan in the freezer. Stir the cider every 30 minutes using a stiff wire whisk or large fork. Continue to do this every 30 minutes until the cider is fully frozen and will form a ball when scooped. The ice should be somewhat fluffy and look like shaved glass.

Keep the granita frozen until you're ready to serve. Then scoop it into a martini glass or a cool bowl. Garnish with a sprig of chopped mint.

THE GRAPE AND THE BEAN

Until recently in America, coffee and wine were an afterthought to the total dining experience. The overly sweet wines that Americans drank during special-occasion dinners and the freeze-dried versions of bad coffee that manufacturers were trying to foist on us have mercifully lost popularity. People such as Robert Mondavi and companies such as Starbucks have pioneered enormous changes in what we drink. Interestingly, coffee and wine are very similar in that growing methods, harvesting techniques, blending processes, and aging procedures are critical to developing great flavors. Both the grape and the bean occupy mystical and historic places in the history of world food, and the recent adoption of new standards of quality has allowed many of us to enjoy the fruits of development, and to integrate them into menus.

The Mist Grill is partners with a coffee business that operates within the confines of our building. Our resident coffee genius, Mané Alves, runs a coffee-testing and -roasting business in a sleek lab here, and we're the grateful recipients of his endless supply of the finest fresh-roasted beans from around the world. The result is that we serve the best coffee anywhere! We've won awards for the coffee we serve, and our regulars profess they won't settle for anything else. Just like the best winemakers, Mané has developed a certain style at what he does, and has unbelievable skill in selecting and blending the various beans he acquires. The finished product is also carefully brewed under proper guidelines and conditions, and Mané won't allow a pot of coffee to sit for more than twenty minutes.

We also pride ourselves on making the best use of his espresso roasts in our signature cappuccinos, lattés, mochas, and espresso drinks. Careful attention to steaming the milk properly, not overdrawing the espresso so it becomes diluted, and employing the highest-quality hand-shaved chocolate and ground nutmeg all contribute to the proper look and taste of a perfect coffee drink.

We don't have the space at the Mist Grill for a wine cellar, but we've found a way to turn this to a benefit for our customers. Without storage room, we take limited deliveries and turn over the inventory very quickly. The philosophy that my partner, Robin, developed is based on the idea that if we don't mark up the wines as much as other restaurants do, and if we provide a unique selection, we'll sell lots of wine. Robin's theory has proved immensely successful, and we do sell gallons of wine. We never charge more than $30, and most customers recognize that with prices this good, they can't afford *not* to try something. Robin also spends hours searching for wines that complement the food we serve. As a result, the list is educational and not intimidating. All of our service staff feel comfortable suggesting a wine to accompany any dish.

It obviously takes time to learn about wines, and this learning never is over. The only way to learn about wine is to taste as much as possible and learn to recognize styles, regions, and flavors. Tasting wine is very subjective; you may find a wine you love, while the person next to you can't stand it. I say, if you like the wine then it *is* great. Many people simply shy away from wine because they don't want to make the wrong choice, or are intimidated by too many choices and have been led to believe that the only good wines are the expensive ones! I always encourage people to relax about wine and feel free to admit they know little. Be honest about it, and the people who work in good wine shops and restaurants will go out of their way to make you feel comfortable and assist you in choosing a wine. If they don't, then take your business to a place where they actually want to help you and sell wine.

During the 1980s I was chef for Banfi Vintners at its corporate offices in Long Island—a magnificent restored Gold Coast mansion. Here I got to prepare elaborate lunches and dinners for chefs, restaurateurs, food writers, and wine professionals. Most functions featured eight- to ten-course tasting menus, with each course paired with Banfi wines. It was through the mentoring of Banfi's winemaster Lucio Sorre that I came to learn the art of pairing wine with food. It's an especially challenging way to cook, since it demands creating dishes that complement a particular wine, whereas in restaurants, people generally pick the wine to match the food. It was through using this reverse approach that I came to understand the subtle ways wine and food change when paired. I could spend several chapters on the subject, but the most important lesson I can share is this: Wine needs food more than food needs wine.

For example, imagine drinking a glass of monstrous Brunello di Montalcino by itself. This wine is so big, some people might have a difficult time drinking the entire glass without food. When the same wine is served with a rack of lamb that has a caramelized flavor, rich marbled fat, and a savory saltiness, however, it reacts with the fats and tannins, and its overpowering flavors are mellowed. Even a simple taste of aged blue cheese or Parmigiano Reggiano can demonstrate how food balances a wine's power. (These cheeses, by the way, are what I often served with the Brunello.)

Still, wine is usually purchased to match a particular dish. It would be hard for me to sit down and eat a steak without a full-bodied Cabernet, or a roasted duck without a juicy Pinot Noir, or (my favorite combination in the world) rack of lamb with fine Bordeaux! There are so many good and reasonably priced wines to choose from now that it's difficult to keep up. Most wines are produced now to be consumed within two years of purchase, so don't think that all wine must be aged longer.

Regardless of the wines you choose to enjoy, wine should be recognized for its social powers as well. Wine has for centuries represented celebration and a sense of peace and well-being. The alcohol content certainly is responsible for some of those properties, but the transformation from grape to wine is somewhat magical. Every bottle is its own time capsule. I love to imagine what the day was like when the cork was placed in the bottle, and then pulling the cork and releasing the wee bit of atmosphere from two or five or even fifty years ago!

Our food at the Mist Grill goes well with wine, and the relaxed feeling of a county dinner is greatly enhanced with a bottle of wine. Picture the snow falling outside, soft candlelight, and the aroma of roasting meats wafting by as you inhale the bouquet of a Syrah . . . and then realize that things are meant to be this way—good food, good wine, and good company.

Some basic hints that apply to both the grape and the bean can help you get the most enjoyment from them. Most important, oxygen is no friend to either. When storing coffee try to eliminate any air in the container. There are some great devices that have a valve and a pump to remove all air from the container. (The very same principle can be used to "recork" bottles of wine with a device called a Vac-U-Vin.) Many people think that storing coffee in the freezer helps to insure freshness. True, this helps slow down the process of oxidation, but if there is air in the container it actually makes it worse because it will form ice crystals that damage the beans.

It is also very important to grind the beans just prior to brewing so the ground coffee sees as little exposure to air as possible. Be sure to grind the coffee to the right size: too small and it will cake up when wet and possibly cause the brewer to overflow, too large and you won't provide enough surface area to extract the flavor and oils from the beans. A little practice and you will find the right balance to meet your preference.

It's easy to get caught up in all the coffee toys for brewing, grinding, storing, steaming, and more, most of which are completely unnecessary, but one device worth investing in is a French coffee press—a glass carafe with a mesh strainer that you plunge to force the coffee to the bottom of the container once it's brewed. The simplicity of the brew method provides a perfect cup of coffee, because the hot water is in direct contact with the grinds long enough to extract maximum flavor. The only drawback is that even the largest model only holds about 3 large cups of coffee, but the results are worth having to brew a few consecutive pots when you've got a crowd.

Drip filter brewers like the Mr. Coffee type will brew a decent pot of coffee, but make sure the grind size is right for the machine and filter you are using, and be sure to use the right amount of coffee to begin with.

The type of bean and its origin are also important, but as with wine, some like Merlot others Cabernet. Taste the various styles of roasts and types of beans before you preclude any particular region or style. The beans all have different flavor nuances. You can detect berry notes, floral aromas, earthy tones, and even fruit flavors. Once you get into it, you may discover that coffee tasting is as exciting and endlessly varied as wine tasting!

As with coffees, the environmental influences of the vineyards will be apparent in the flavor of wines. A subtle hint of eucalyptus or honey, stronger berry notes or floral characteristics—this will all be more or less pronounced at times, depending on the maturity of the grapes and the practices taken by the winemaker. I am far from a wine expert but have had years of experience tasting and pairing wines and food. I've learned that there really are no hard rules, except this one: wines don't necessarily get better with age or price! So don't spend a fortune, and don't bother cellaring wines for years. Just drink a lot of different wines with all types of food until you start to learn what works for you and what doesn't. Explore, explore, explore, and don't forget to enjoy the process—that's the whole point, after all.

THE BASIC COMFORTS

As a professional chef, I am continually asked the question, "What do you cook when you're at home?" Most of the time, unless we are entertaining, Robin and I will make some of the most basic stuff imaginable. Exotic ingredients and adventurous dishes are great, and are why I never get bored running a restaurant, but after all that work sometimes you just want the simple flavors that you know work every time. They are not always fast recipes, but dishes like slow-cooked roasts or casseroles that are in the oven for several hours provide tantalizing aromas throughout the day, leading up to that great moment when the lid is removed and you can barely resist tearing into the crisp layer on a pot roast or the moist leg of a roast chicken.

This is what rustic is all about. I often wonder about the days when there was no electricity and the dinner bell would ring for the family to gather for supper. After incredible manual labor and building hunger throughout the day, what could be better than sitting down to beef that falls apart with the touch of a fork, vegetables that have been transformed to caramelized nuggets of flavor, warm biscuits, corn just brought in from the fields, and maybe a hearty ale from the root cellar. There is something in all of us that hearkens back to those times, and for that part of us sometimes a well-made, hearty dish is just the thing to make us feel that all is right with the world. The following recipes are for when that yearning takes a hold of you.

Blush Hill Pot Roast

Makes 6 to 8 servings

Sunday Suppers at the Mist Grill is the time when you will find the smells of a slow-cooking pot roast. Cooked for hours, the beef becomes infused with rich natural juices. Blush Hill is the road Robin and I live on.

Prior to opening the Mist Grill, we hosted many dinner parties, both fancy and informal, and our friends referred to these soirees as the Blush Hill Restaurant. This pot roast was featured at more than one such event.

INGREDIENTS

3 to 5 pounds beef, bottom round

16 garlic cloves

4 chipotle peppers in adobo

12 ounces dark beer (stout or porter)

2 cups veal stock

8 carrots, peeled

8 parsnips

12 small red-skin potatoes

2 fennel bulbs, quartered

8 celery stalks

2 onions sliced ½-inch thick

PREPARATION

Preheat the oven to 350 degrees.

In a large cast-iron Dutch oven or roasting pan, add enough vegetable oil to just coat the pan. Trim the beef of excess fat, but do not overtrim as the fat will be key to the finished flavor of the dish. Liberally season the meat with salt and pepper.

Heat the pan on high until the oil is hot. Place the beef in the pan and brown the entire surface evenly. Add the garlic and peppers and cook for 1 minute.

Add the beer and veal stock and then place the vegetables around the beef, saving the onion slices for last and placing them on top of the beef as much as possible. Cover the pan with the lid or tightly with foil wrap.

Place the pan in the oven and roast for 2½ hours.

Remove the vegetables and place on an ovenproof serving platter or casserole dish.

Pour all the pan juices into a clean pot and let sit for 5 minutes to let any fat rise to the surface. Skim off the fat and bring the liquid to a boil, reduce the heat and simmer for 10 to 15 minutes. You can use a roux to thicken the sauce if desired, but I prefer a lighter sauce.

Slice the beef as thinly as possible and serve with the assortment of vegetables and the sauce ladled over the top. Be sure to have some good crusty bread on hand for soaking up the juices!

Slow Roast Chicken

Makes 4 servings

There may be 1001 ways to prepare chicken, but as far as I am concerned plain old roasted chicken is the number one way to go. There is something about great roasted chicken that is hard to beat. Restaurant chains have been built around roasted chicken and for good cause. Totally satisfying in all departments, it is a dependable dish that everyone enjoys. I have joked to several flavor companies we work with that they should bottle the aroma of roasted chicken and sell it as perfume for those with a real hankering for home cooking!

The only dish at the Mist Grill that hasn't changed at all since we opened is the chicken we serve every Sunday Supper. This version is similar, but different in that it is cooked covered for some time before the lid is removed to brown the skin.

INGREDIENTS

4 to 5 pound roaster chicken

1 tablespoon celery salt

1 teaspoon black pepper

1 tablespoon salt

1 lemon, cut into ¼-inch-thick slices

6 garlic cloves

1 onion, sliced thin

4 carrots, halved lengthwise

4 celery stalks

PREPARATION

Preheat oven to 300 degrees.

Remove the neck and giblets and wash the bird well with cold water. Season evenly with the celery salt, pepper, and salt. Place the lemon and garlic cloves in the cavity of the bird.

Place the bird in a roasting pan and arrange all the vegetables around it. Cover tightly with foil wrap and cook in the oven for 1½ hours.

Increase the temperature to 350 degrees and remove the foil wrap. Cook for ½ hour more until the skin is evenly browned.

Remove the vegetables and place them in a casserole dish. Remove the bird and cut it into leg, thigh, and breast pieces. Serve immediately with some of the pan juices poured over the chicken.

Boiled Dinner

Makes 4 servings

Most people only think about corned beef on St. Patrick's Day, but, in New England in particular, the other 364 days of the year are all excellent candidates to have a pot boiling away filled with a hearty mix of root vegetables, cabbage, and beef brisket. The classic New England boiled dinner is just that, and sometimes there is nothing more satisfying than sitting down with a great beer and a crock of good strong mustard to anoint the sliced meat and tender veggies. It doesn't get much more rustic than that!

INGREDIENTS

3- to 4-pound corned beef brisket

6 garlic cloves

4 bay leaves

12 peppercorns

2 bottles cheap beer

12 red-skin potatoes

8 carrots, peeled

1 head green cabbage, quartered

PREPARATION

Place the brisket in a large stockpot and fill the pot with 3 quarts of water. Add the garlic cloves, bay leaves, peppercorns, and beer. Bring to a boil, then reduce the heat to a simmer. Cover the pot and cook for 1 hour.

Add the potatoes and carrots. Cook, covered, for 20 minutes.

Add the cabbage, making sure it is submerged. Cook, covered, for 10 minutes, until the cabbage is just tender.

Remove all the ingredients and place on a large serving platter. Slice the meat across the grain as thinly as possible and serve immediately.

The Ploughman's Lunch

Makes 1 serving

Our simplest dish! No cooking required, just an assembly of great ingredients that compliment each other and lead to great satisfaction. We have kept it on the menu from day one, as we have a dedicated following who practically live on it.

Dating back to farming days, the ploughman's lunch consists of pâtés, cheeses, pickles, and crusty bread. It evolved as something the farmer could throw together without taking much time away from the fields or having to find a source of fire to cook.

We like to present the ingredients on variations of a "platter," such as pieces of slate or small cutting boards. Think rustic! There is no definitive selection of the ingredients and we constantly change them. Some days the platter will have sharp Cheddar or goat cheese, some days Stilton. We change the pâtés as well but usually always serve a country-style one.

INGREDIENTS

2 slices pâté de campagne

1 slice mousse de foie gras

2 slices sharp Vermont Cheddar

2 ounces chevre

6 cornichons

1 apple, sliced in wedges

4 thick slices French bread

1 tablespoon Dijon mustard

1 tablespoon coarse grain mustard

PREPARATION

Slice all the ingredients and arrange them on a platter of choice, keeping enough space between all of them so they are not touching and have some artistic definition. Serve immediately.

One-Pan Pasta Rustica

Makes 6 to 8 servings

Every day we cook something for the staff to eat before dinner service or after the lunch shift. The kitchen is always busy getting ready for service or breaking down after lunch and cooking something at those times can be a pain. Staff meal is always comprised of "stuff" and pasta is a great way to incorporate various stuff and call it something fun. The truth is that leftovers are the foundation for most of the staff meals, but I specialize in making quick and hearty *rusticas* that everyone seems to enjoy—as long as I don't make it several days in a row! This is a great way to clean out the fridge.

PREPARATION

Bring a large pot of water to a boil. Add the pasta and cook to al dente doneness, about 10–12 minutes. Rinse with cool water and set aside.

Preheat the oven to 350 degrees.

Cook the ground beef in a large skillet for 8 to10 minutes until browned. Drain off half the liquid and fat.

Add the onions, garlic, and peppers and cook for 5 to 8 minutes or until the onions are translucent. Add the tomatoes and olives and cook for 5 minutes while stirring.

INGREDIENTS

1 pound dry pasta (any will do, but I prefer penne for this dish)

1 pound ground beef

1 cup shaved onions

2 garlic cloves, minced

1 cup red pepper, diced

1 cup green pepper, diced

32 ounces canned crushed tomatoes

½ cup olives, pitted and chopped

1 cup Mozzarela cheese, shredded

1 cup Bleu cheese, crumbled

2 teaspoons basil, dried

1 teaspoon oregano, dried

2 teaspoons salt

2 teaspoons black pepper

Add the cooked pasta and the salt and pepper, toss well, then flatten all the ingredients by compressing them. Sprinkle all the cheese over the pasta and place in the oven.

Bake the dish for 10 to 12 minutes or until the cheese is fully melted and starts to bubble. Serve immediately.

Sunday Morning Santa Fe Frittata

Makes 6 to 8 servings

Being in the restaurant business tends to drastically change your lifestyle whcn it comes to free time. Sunday morning is one of the rare times left to kick back, get the paper, and have a leisurely breakfast. Having cooked all week I personally don't want to spend too much time in the kitchen fussing with lots of ingredients or dealing with a sink full of pots and pans. That's where a frittata comes in handy.

This Frittata is particularly flexible and easy. Almost any ingredient goes. I like a Tex-Mex version because it lets me use up that jar of salsa in the fridge.

INGREDIENTS

12 large eggs

2 tablespoons vegetable oil

1 cup onions, diced

1 cup red peppers, diced

2 tablespoons jalapenos, minced

½ cup salsa

2 tablespoons cilantro, minced

1 cup Monterey Jack or Cheddar cheese, shredded

PREPARATION

Preheat the oven to 450 degrees.

Crack the eggs into a bowl and whisk well.

In a 12-inch nonstick skillet, add the oil, turn the heat to high, and add all the vegetables. Sauté for 3 to 4 minutes, then add the salsa and cilantro.

Add the eggs and very quickly stir them into the vegetable mixture. Cook for 1 minute while stirring until the eggs just begin to set.

Place the pan in the oven and bake for 10 minutes or until the eggs have puffed up like a soufflé. Carefully remove the pan and sprinkle the cheese evenly over the top of the eggs. Place back in the oven and cook for 3 to 5 minutes until the cheese is melted and just begins to brown on the edges.

Remove the pan and let the frittata cool for 2 minutes.

Carefully slice the frittata like a cake and serve the wedges immediately.

Roast Leg of Lamb

Makes 6 to 8 servings

Nothing fancy about a roast leg of lamb, but it rates very high on my list of favorite comfort dinners. Thankfully, the days of cooking lamb until well done are long over; when cooked properly to a medium or medium rare, leg of lamb is outstanding.

The goal with leg of lamb is to get a good caramelized outer crust and a nice juicy pink center. The fat content and base flavor of lamb provide plenty of savor on their own, so I keep the seasonings simple. Serve this roast with a hearty side dish such as the Israeli Couscous Risotto or the Pan-Mashed Potatoes. Find a big red wine such as a Brunello or Barolo and enjoy!

INGREDIENTS

6 sprigs fresh rosemary

20 garlic cloves, peeled

¼ cup olive oil

2 tablespoons black pepper

2 tablespoons salt

4-pound boneless leg of lamb

PREPARATION

Preheat the oven to 275 degrees.

Strip the leaves from the rosemary sprigs and place them in a food processor with the garlic, olive oil, pepper, and salt. Process until coarsely pureed.

Unroll the lamb and evenly coat the inside of the meat with about a quarter of the puree. Roll the lamb back to its original roast size and evenly coat the entire leg of lamb with the remaining puree. Place in a roasting pan with the seam side down.

Roast the lamb in the oven until well browned and the internal temperature reaches 130 degrees for rare or 140 for medium. Depending on the actual weight of the roast it should cook for approximately 2 to 2½ hours. It is important to check the temperature using a meat thermometer to insure accuracy in doneness. During the cooking time, regularly open the oven and baste the lamb with the pan juices as they develop.

Remove the lamb from the oven and let it cool for 10 minutes. Slice and serve with any remaining pan juices.

Stevie and Kirsten's Caramelized Apple French Toast

Makes 4 servings

I am a firm believer in getting kids into the kitchen as often as possible. They should be exposed to different foods and to cooking at an early age. The majority of the children today exist on fast food and don't have the vaguest idea what many foods are like or where they come from. My kids had no choice in the matter, as they have virtually grown up in and around the kitchen. They have become quite proficient in the kitchen and can make some fantastic meals on their own. One of the first dishes Stevie and Kirsten collaborated on was when they decided to take the lead on making breakfast one Sunday and surprise Robin and I with their creation.

Like most kids, they have a sweet tooth, so they improvised by making a version of Apple Tarte Tatin that they had helped make before, and paired it with good old French toast. It has become one of our favorite Sunday morning treats.

INGREDIENTS

2 tablespoons butter, plus more for sautéing French toast

6 apples, peeled and thinly sliced

1 cup sugar

½ cup maple syrup

1 tablespoon cinnamon

1 tablespoon vanilla

4 eggs

2 cups milk

8 slices whole wheat bread

PREPARATION

In a large sauté pan heat the butter and add the apples. Sauté for 4 to 5 minutes over medium heat until they start to become soft. Remove the apples and place them in a bowl.

Add the sugar and maple syrup to the pan and cook over medium heat until the sugar is fully dissolved and it begins to boil and become deep brown.

Add the apple back to the pan and add the cinnamon and vanilla. Continue to cook and stir for 1 minute. Reduce the heat to very low and hold until ready to use.

Crack the eggs in a bowl. Add the milk and whisk well.

Dip the bread one slice at a time, let it absorb the egg mixture for a few seconds, and place in a buttered hot skillet. Fit as many slices as you can in the pan without crowding them.

Cook the toast over medium heat until the underside is golden, then flip and cook the other side.

Serve immediately with a healthy spoonful of the apple syrup. If you can get your kids to deliver it to your bedside, all the better!

Balsamic Vinaigrette

Makes 1½ cups

This is my favorite and simplest dressing recipe; even my children whip it up, and they never measure anything. You'll see it called for in several of this book's recipes.

PREPARATION

Combine the oil, vinegar, Dijon mustard, basil, salt, and pepper in a mixing bowl. Whisk vigorously until the dressing is completely blended and deep mahogany in color. Set aside in a clean container or refrigerate until needed.

INGREDIENTS

1 cup olive oil

⅓ cup balsamic vinegar

3 tablespoons Dijon mustard

1 tablespoon finely minced fresh basil

½ teaspoon salt

½ teaspoon pepper

STOCKS AND CRUSTS

I know, I know. I said don't bother making your own. But there are still some people out there who are willing to make that commitment to turning out the absolutely most authentic food possible. If you're one of those hardcore cooks, these recipes are for you.

Veal Stock

Makes 3 to 4 quarts

Good veal stock is one of the most versatile and important stocks to have on hand in any kitchen. It is very simple to make but requires some patience. You should make a large amount at once and freeze it to really make it worth your while. The aroma alone, as it is simmering for hours, will make you happy you took the time to make stock.

Veal stock is also the beginning of what becomes demiglace. Demiglace is simply veal stock that is reduced to about half its original volume. Depending on the intensity and rich-ness of the first stock, the amount you need to reduce it is somewhat subjective. I will some-times reduce the stock by as much as 75 per-cent in an effort to gain more depth of flavor and texture. One of the ultimate sauces in the world is when veal stock has been reduced to the point where it becomes syrup and coats your lips with a sweet and sticky glaze! I usu-ally finish the demiglace with a small amount of butter, which adds that extra bit of fat and mouth feel to the sauce, as well as rounding out the savory components of the veal stock.

INGREDIENTS

¼ cup vegetable oil

8 pounds veal bones

3 large onions (cut in quarters with skin on)

3 cups diced celery

3 cups carrots (peeled and rough chopped)

3 cups crushed canned tomatoes

8 cloves garlic (peeled and smashed)

3 bay leaves

1 teaspoon dried thyme

2 teaspoons kosher salt

12 black peppercorns

PREPARATION

Preheat the oven to 350 degrees.

Add the vegetable oil to a large roasting pan and place the veal bones in the pan as evenly as possible. Roast the bones for 45 minutes, then remove the pan from the oven.

Add all the celery, onions, carrots, and tomatoes and blend as well as possible. Place the pan back in the oven and cook for 30 minutes.

Remove the pan from the oven and care-fully transfer the contents to a large stockpot. Add all the other ingredients and enough water to completely cover the ingredients with 1 inch extra.

Bring the stock to a full boil and then reduce the heat to simmer. Simmer the stock for 8 hours, adding water as needed to keep the ingredients covered. During the simmer

continued next page

time use a large spoon or ladle to skim any foam or fat off the top.

Remove from the heat and let the stock cool for 30 to 60 minutes so you can strain it without getting burned. To strain the stock, layer the inside of a strainer with cheesecloth to better catch the fine solids. Use a pair of tongs to remove the veal bones and discard them—or give the family pooch a real treat!

Carefully pour the stock through the strainer into a clean large container. Be sure to get every drop of liquid, and discard the other ingredients.

You can store the stock in smaller containers and keep frozen for up to 6 months.

To make demiglace, heat the stock and simmer until it is reduced to half of its original volume.

Chicken Stock

Makes 3 to 4 quarts

Just like veal stock, chicken stock is a superbly versatile ingredient for thousands of dishes. Chicken stock can be as simple as throwing the remnants of a carved bird and some vegetables into water and letting it boil for an hour. At the Mist Grill, I prefer to roast the bones and chicken before adding any water, as the roasting develops a richer, deeper, caramelized stock with more identity. As with any stock, it is a good idea to make enough to be able to freeze some for spontaneous use later on.

You can use any parts of the chicken, including neck and gizzards. When we make this stock we remove most of the meat and cook it separately for other uses, and for the stock use the bones with whatever meat is still attached.

INGREDIENTS

4 pounds raw chicken (wings and bones with meat still attached)

2 large onions, quartered with skins on

1½ cups carrots, chopped

2 cups celery, with tops, chopped

1 teaspoon peppercorns

1 tablespoon minced fresh sage

PREPARATION

Preheat the oven to 350 degrees.

Place the chicken in a roasting pan and roast for 45 minutes.

Remove the chicken and place in a large stockpot. Add all the remaining ingredients and enough water to cover them with one inch extra. Bring the stock to a full boil and then reduce to a medium simmer and continue to cook for 2 hours.

Remove the pot from the heat and let it cool enough to handle safely. Slowly strain the stock through a strainer lined with cheesecloth into a clean pot.

Skim any solids, fat, or foam off the top and bring to a boil. Reduce the heat to a simmer and continue to cook for 30 minutes.

Store the stock in small containers and use within 3 days or freeze for up to 6 months.

Pie Crust

Makes 4 crusts

Come on, it ain't that hard!

INGREDIENTS

8 tablespoons (one stick) cold unsalted butter; diced

8 tablespoons cold vegetable shortening

3 cups all-purpose flour

1½ teaspoons salt

1½ teaspoons sugar

⅓ cup plus 2 tablespoons ice water

PREPARATION

Place the diced butter and shortening in the freezer while you prepare the flour and water. Fill a 2-cup measuring cup with ice cubes and water. Set aside. Put the flour, salt, and sugar in the bowl of a food processor and process to mix. Add the butter and shortening in pieces. Give the machine about twenty quick pulses until the mixture is the consistency of cornmeal with pea-sized pieces of butter.

Measure out the ice water. Pour about half the measured ice water into the bottom of a large mixing bowl. Dump the flour mixture over it and sprinkle the remaining water over the top. Using both hands, toss the dough to evenly moisten. Squeeze a handful of dough: if it clumps together it is moist enough; if not, sprinkle on a little more water and toss.

Turn the dough out onto the table, scraping the bowl well and, with the heel of your hand, gently mash the dough into the table with a few quick strokes. Gather the dough together into a rough log shape. Score it in four equal pieces and cut it so that it is divided into 4 equal pieces. Wrap each in plastic wrap and chill for four hours or overnight.

When ready to use, place a disc of dough on a floured surface and roll to a diameter of 12 inches. If necessary, loosen it from the table using a long flexible metal spatula. Brush off any excess flour, fold the circle in half, center it over a 9-inch glass pie plate and open it. Gently mold the dough down and around the sides without stretching it. Using a paring knife, cut the excess dough around the rim so that it is flush with the edge of the pie plate. For a pie that requires a top crust, repeat the process with another dough disk and crimp the bottom and top crusts together to seal the edges well. The dough will freeze for several weeks if each piece is individually wrapped well in advance.

INDEX

Aged Cheddar and Heavy Cream Grits, 64

appetizers, 37–56

    Cappelini alla Black Walnut, 45

    Doug's Coconut Tuna Ceviche, 54

    Grilled Shrimp on Creamy Grits with Tomato Chili Puree, 43–44

    Oven-Roasted Portabella with Corn and Roasted Garlic Flan, 55–56

    Purple Potato *Causa* Topped with Pulled Chicken, 48–49

    Salmon and Tuna Sashimi Towers with Wasabi Cream and Sesame Oil, 50

    Smoked Trout Cakes with Horseradish Crème Fraîche, 41–42

    Thai Peanut Butter and Jelly with Mesclun, 46–47

    Tomato-Mozzarella Club with Basil and Balsamic Syrup, 51

    Warm Stilton Flan with Grilled Pears and Brown Bread, 39–40

    Wild Mushroom and Goat Cheese Tartlets, 52–53

apples, 115

    Apple and Bourbon Bread Pudding, 125

    Apple Cider and Dried Cranberry Granita, 130

    Apple Crisp Pie with Sharp Cheddar, 129

    Bea's Firecracker Apple Fritters, 69

    Jason's Apple Crisp Salmon with Wilted Greens and Reduced Cider, 100

    Maple-Glazed Oven-Roasted Chicken with Grilled Apple Hash, 103

    Open Apple Croustade with Cinnamon Cream, 128

    The Ploughman's Lunch, 146

    Stevie and Kirsten's Caramelized Apple French Toast, 150

apricots

    Roasted Half Duck with Marinated Apricots and Lingonberry Demiglace, 98–99

arugula

    Summer Tomatoes with Arugula and Steve's Spiced Pecans, 33

bacon

    Oven-Roasted Cod with Clam Chowder Broth, 90

    Stevie's Alfredo Carbonara, 106

    Summer Pea Salad, 81

barley

    Pan-Roasted Monkfish with Lobster Stock and Barley, 96–97

Bea's Firecracker Apple Fritters, 69

beans

    Roasted Tomato, White Bean, and Spinach Soup, 77

    Smoky and Spicy Black Beans, 68

beef
    Black Cherry and Chipotle Baby Back Ribs, 94
    Blush Hill Pot Roast, 143
    Boiled Dinner, 145
    Grilled Ribeye of Beef with Blue Cheese Butter and
        Tomato Cruda, 91–92
    Grilled Veal Chop with Wild Mushroom Ragout
        and Truffled Demiglace, 110
    One-Pan Pasta Rustica, 147
    stock, 157–58
berries
    Apple Cider and Dried Cranberry Granita, 130
    Lemon Curd Sandwich with Berry Sauce, 123–24
    Summer Fruit Strudel, 127
Bibb Lettuce with Toasted Pistachios and Goat Cheese,
    30–31
Black Cherry and Chipotle Baby Back Ribs, 94
Blush Hill Pot Roast, 143
Boiled Dinner, 145
bread
    The Ploughman's Lunch, 146
    Stevie and Kirsten's Caramelized Apple French
        Toast, 150
    Thai Peanut Butter and Jelly with Mesclun, 46–47
    Warm Stilton Flan with Grilled Pears and Brown
        Bread, 39–40
cabbage
    Boiled Dinner, 145
    Poppy Seed Kraut, 93
    Thai Cole Slaw, 82
Cappelini alla Black Walnut, 45
cheese
    Aged Cheddar and Heavy Cream Grits, 64
    Bibb Lettuce with Toasted Pistachios and Goat
        Cheese, 30–31
    Cherry Tomatoes with Goat Cheese, Cracked
        Pepper, and Honey Drizzle, 15
    Grilled Ribeye of Beef with Blue Cheese Butter and
        Tomato Cruda, 91–92
    Apple Crisp Pie with Sharp Cheddar, 129
    One-Pan Pasta Rustica, 147
    The Ploughman's Lunch, 146
    Risotto Cakes with Asiago Gratin, 67
    Robin's "I Invented It" Mac and Cheese, 80, 89
    The Steak House Wedge, 32
    Summer Vegetable and Portabella Napoleon, 108
    Sunday Morning Santa Fe Frittata, 148
    Tomato-Mozzarella Club with Basil and Balsamic
        Syrup, 51

Vegetable Spoon Explosions, 16
Warm Spinach with Pan-Roasted Pears and Stilton,
    29
Warm Stilton Flan with Grilled Pears and Brown
    Bread, 39–40
Wild Mushroom and Goat Cheese Tartlets, 52–53
cherries
    Black Cherry and Chipotle Baby Back Ribs, 94
Cherry Tomatoes with Goat Cheese, Cracked Pepper,
    and Honey Drizzle, 15
chicken
    Chicken Saltimboca Sinatra, 107
    Maple-Glazed Oven-Roasted Chicken with Grilled
        Apple Hash, 103
    Purple Potato Causa Topped with Pulled Chicken,
        48–49
    Sea Salt and Sage Crusted Chicken with Pearl
        Onion Gravy, 89
    Slow Roast Chicken, 144
    stock, 159
chocolate
    Chocolate Almond Torte, 122
    sauce, 121
coconut
    Corn Chowder with Shrimp and Green Chilies, 76
    Doug's Coconut Tuna Ceviche, 54
coffee, 135–38
cooking
    ingredients, selecting, 6–7
    rustic, 3–6, 141
corn
    Aged Cheddar and Heavy Cream Grits, 64
    Creamy Chipotle Polenta, 78
    Grilled Shrimp on Creamy Grits with Tomato Chili
        Puree, 43–44
    Mini Grilled Polenta Sandwich, 21–22
    Oven-Roasted Portabella with Corn and Roasted
        Garlic Flan, 55–56
    Summer Fair Dipped Corn on the Cob, 79
Corn Chowder with Shrimp and Green Chilies, 76
couscous
    Israeli Couscous Risotto-Style, 71
    Robin's "I Invented It" Mac and Cheese, 80, 89
Crab and Caviar Bomblets, 17
Cream of Portabella, 74
Creamy Chipotle Polenta, 78
Crème Brûlée, 117
Dave Burke's Roasted Pork Shank with Poppy Seed
    Kraut, 93

desserts, 115–30
    Apple and Bourbon Bread Pudding, 125
    Apple Cider and Dried Cranberry Granita, 130
    Apple Crisp Pie with Sharp Cheddar, 129
    Chocolate Almond Torte, 122
    Gingerbread Bomb, 120–21
    Lemon Curd Sandwich with Berry Sauce, 123–24
    Open Apple Croustade with Cinnamon Cream,
       128
    Peach and Basil Ice Cream, 126
    Pear and Ginger Tarte Tatin with Allspice Anglaise,
       118–19
    Summer Fruit Strudel, 127
    Vermont Maple Crème Brûlée, 117
Dijon-Crusted Rack of Lamb, 101
Doug's Coconut Tuna Ceviche, 54
dressings
    balsamic vinaigrette, 33, 48, 151
    blood orange vinaigrette, 28
    cranberry vinaigrette, 29
    orange soy, 46–47
    roasted red pepper, 30–31
    sherry vinaigrette, 27
duck
    Roasted Half Duck with Marinated Apricots and
       Lingonberry Demiglace, 98–99
eggplant
    Grilled Ratatouille, 70
eggs
    Sunday Morning Santa Fe Frittata, 148
fennel
    Shaved Fennel and Parmesan with Prosciutto, 28
fish
    Corn Chowder with Shrimp and Green Chilies, 76
    Crab and Caviar Bomblets, 17
    Doug's Coconut Tuna Ceviche, 54
    Grilled Shrimp on Creamy Grits with Tomato Chili
       Puree, 43–44
    Grilled Yellowfin Tuna with Summer Tomato
       Cruda, 95
    Jason's Apple Crisp Salmon with Wilted Greens and
       Reduced Cider, 100
    Lobster Latté, 72–73
    Oven-Roasted Cod with Clam Chowder Broth, 90
    Pan-Roasted Monkfish with Lobster Stock and
       Barley, 96–97
    Salmon and Tuna Sashimi Towers with Wasabi
       Cream and Sesame Oil, 50

Shrimp Churascaritas with Cilantro Chimichurri à
    la Kirsten, 104–5
Shrimp Tarte Tatin with Roasted Tomatoes and
    Calamata Olives, 109
Smoked Trout Cakes with Horseradish Crème
    Fraîche, 41–42
Tomato-Poached Shrimp, 20
flan
    Oven-Roasted Portabella with Corn and Roasted
       Garlic Flan, 55–56
    Warm Stilton Flan with Grilled Pears and Brown
       Bread, 39–40
Gingerbread Bomb, 120–21
gingerroot
    Pear and Ginger Tarte Tatin with Allspice Anglaise,
       118–19
granita, 130
Grilled Ratatouille, 70
Grilled Ribeye of Beef with Blue Cheese Butter and
    Tomato Cruda, 91–92
Grilled Shrimp on Creamy Grits with Tomato Chili
    Puree, 43–44
Grilled Veal Chop with Wild Mushroom Ragout and
    Truffled Demiglace, 110
Grilled Yellowfin Tuna with Summer Tomato Cruda, 95
hors d'oeuvres, 13–22
    Cherry Tomatoes with Goat Cheese, Cracked
       Pepper, and Honey Drizzle, 15
    Crab and Caviar Bomblets, 17
    Mini Grilled Polenta Sandwich, 21–22
    Oven-Roasted Balsamic Olives, 18
    Savory Palmiers with English Mustard, 19
    Tomato-Poached Shrimp, 20
    Vegetable Spoon Explosions, 16
ice cream
    Peach and Basil Ice Cream, 126
Israeli Couscous Risotto-Style, 71
Jason's Apple Crisp Salmon with Wilted Greens and
    Reduced Cider, 100
Killer Rösti Potatoes, 63
lamb
    Dijon-Crusted Rack of Lamb, 101
    Roast Leg of Lamb, 149
lemon
    Lemon Curd Sandwich with Berry Sauce, 123–24
Like Water for Chocolate, 4
lingonberries
    demiglace, 98–99

Lobster Latté, 72–73

mango
    Thai Cole Slaw, 82
Maple-Glazed Oven-Roasted Chicken with Grilled
    Apple Hash, 103
Mini Grilled Polenta Sandwich, 21–22
Mist Greens with Robin's Sherry Vinaigrette, 27
Mist Grill, The, 3–4, 7–9
mushrooms
    Cream of Portabella, 74
    Grilled Veal Chop with Wild Mushroom Ragout
        and Truffled Demiglace, 110
    Mushroom Cappuccino, 75
    Mushroom Tarte Tatin with Parmesan Anglaise and
        Truffle Oil, 102
    Oven-Roasted Portabella with Corn and Roasted
        Garlic Flan, 55–56
    Summer Vegetable and Portabella Napoleon, 108
    Wild Mushroom and Goat Cheese Tartlets, 52–53
nuts
    Bibb Lettuce with Toasted Pistachios and Goat
        Cheese, 30–31
    Chocolate Almond Torte, 122
    Summer Tomatoes with Arugula and Steve's Spiced
        Pecans, 33
    Thai Peanut Butter and Jelly with Mesclun, 46–47
olives
    Oven-Roasted Balsamic Olives, 18
    Shrimp Tarte Tatin with Roasted Tomatoes and
        Calamata Olives, 109
One-Pan Pasta Rustica, 147
Open Apple Croustade with Cinnamon Cream, 128
oranges
    orange soy dressing, 46–47
Oven-Roasted Balsamic Olives, 18
Oven-Roasted Cod with Clam Chowder Broth, 90
Oven-Roasted Portabella with Corn and Roasted
    Garlic Flan, 55–56
Pan-Mashed Potatoes, 65
Pan-Roasted Monkfish with Lobster Stock and Barley,
    96–97
parsnips
    Blush Hill Pot Roast, 143
pasta
    Cappelini alla Black Walnut, 45
    One-Pan Pasta Rustica, 147
    Stevie's Alfredo Carbonara, 106

pastry. *See also* desserts
    Mushroom Tarte Tatin with Parmesan Anglaise and
        Truffle Oil, 102
    Savory Palmiers with English Mustard, 19
    Shrimp Tarte Tatin with Roasted Tomatoes and
        Calamata Olives, 109
    Wild Mushroom and Goat Cheese Tartlets, 52–53
pâté
    The Ploughman's Lunch, 146
Peach and Basil Ice Cream, 126
peaches
    Peach and Basil Ice Cream, 126
    Summer Fruit Strudel, 127
pears
    Pear and Ginger Tarte Tatin with Allspice
        Anglaise, 118–19
    Warm Spinach with Pan-Roasted Pears and
        Stilton, 29
    Warm Stilton Flan with Grilled Pears and
        Brown Bread, 39–40
peas
    Summer Pea Salad, 81
peppers
    Grilled Ratatouille, 70
    One-Pan Pasta Rustica, 147
    roasted red pepper dressing, 30–31
    Summer Vegetable and Portabella Napoleon, 108
    Vegetable Spoon Explosions, 16
pie crust, 160
Ploughman's Lunch, The, 146
polenta, 21–22
    Creamy Chipotle Polenta, 78
Poppy Seed Kraut, 93
pork
    Dave Burke's Roasted Pork Shank with Poppy Seed
        Kraut, 93
potatoes, 61
    Blush Hill Pot Roast, 143
    Boiled Dinner, 145
    Corn Chowder with Shrimp and Green Chilies, 76
    Killer Rösti Potatoes, 63
    Oven-Roasted Cod with Clam Chowder Broth, 90
    Pan-Mashed Potatoes, 65
    Purple Potato *Causa* Topped with Pulled Chicken,
        48–49
    Steve's Red Spud Salad with Dijon Dressing, 83
Purple Potato *Causa* Topped with Pulled Chicken,
    48–49

rice
  Risotto Cakes with Asiago Gratin, 67
Roast Leg of Lamb, 149
Roasted Half Duck with Marinated Apricots and
  Lingonberry Demiglace, 98–99
Roasted Tomato, White Bean, and Spinach Soup, 77
Robin's "I Invented It" Mac and Cheese, 80, 89
salads, 25–33. See also dressings
  Bibb Lettuce with Toasted Pistachios and Goat
    Cheese, 30–31
  Mist Greens with Robin's Sherry Vinaigrette, 27
  Shaved Fennel and Parmesan with Prosciutto, 28
  The Steak House Wedge, 32
  Summer Pea Salad, 81
  Summer Tomatoes with Arugula and Steve's Spiced
    Pecans, 33
  Thai Cole Slaw, 82
  Thai Peanut Butter and Jelly with Mesclun, 46–47
  Warm Spinach with Pan-Roasted Pears and
    Stilton, 29
Salmon and Tuna Sashimi Towers with Wasabi Cream
  and Sesame Oil, 50
sauces
  alfredo, 106
  allspice anglaise, 119
  balsamic syrup, 51
  berry, 123–24
  chimichurri, 104–5
  chocolate, 121
  horseradish Crème Fraîche, 41–42
  lingonberry demiglace, 98–99
  tomato chili puree, 43–44
  wasabi cream, 50
Savory Palmiers with English Mustard, 19
Sea Salt and Sage Crusted Chicken with Pearl Onion
  Gravy, 89
Shaved Fennel and Parmesan with Prosciutto, 28
Shrimp Churascaritas with Cilantro Chimichurri à la
  Kirsten, 104–5
Shrimp Tarte Tatin with Roasted Tomatoes and
  Calamata Olives, 109
Slow Roast Chicken, 144
Smoked Trout Cakes with Horseradish Crème Fraîche,
  41–42
Smoky and Spicy Black Beans, 68
soups. See also stocks
  Corn Chowder with Shrimp and Green Chilies, 76
  Cream of Portabella, 74

Lobster Latté, 72–73
Mushroom Cappuccino, 75
Oven-Roasted Cod with Clam Chowder Broth, 90
Pan-Roasted Monkfish with Lobster Stock and
  Barley, 96–97
Roasted Tomato, White Bean, and Spinach
  Soup, 77
spinach
  Jason's Apple Crisp Salmon with Wilted Greens and
    Reduced Cider, 100
  Mini Grilled Polenta Sandwich, 21–22
  Roasted Tomato, White Bean, and Spinach
    Soup, 77
  Summer Vegetable and Portabella Napoleon, 108
  Warm Spinach with Pan-Roasted Pears and
    Stilton, 29
squash
  Grilled Ratatouille, 70
  Summer Vegetable and Portabella Napoleon, 108
Steak House Wedge, The, 32
Stevie's Alfredo Carbonara, 106
Steve's Red Spud Salad with Dijon Dressing, 83
Stevie and Kirsten's Caramelized Apple French
  Toast, 150
stocks. See also soups
  chicken, 159
  veal, 157–58
Summer Fair Dipped Corn on the Cob, 79
Summer Fruit Strudel, 127
Summer Pea Salad, 81
Summer Tomatoes with Arugula and Steve's Spiced
  Pecans, 33
Summer Vegetable and Portabella Napoleon, 108
Sunday Morning Santa Fe Frittata, 148
Swiss chard
  Jason's Apple Crisp Salmon with Wilted Greens
    and Reduced Cider, 100
tableware, 37–38, 87–88
Thai Cole Slaw, 82
Thai Peanut Butter and Jelly with Mesclun, 46–47
tomatoes
  Cappelini alla Black Walnut, 45
  Cherry Tomatoes with Goat Cheese, Cracked
    Pepper, and Honey Drizzle, 15
  Grilled Ratatouille, 70
  Grilled Ribeye of Beef with Blue Cheese Butter and
    Tomato Cruda, 91–92

Grilled Shrimp on Creamy Grits with Tomato Chili Puree, 43

Grilled Yellowfin Tuna with Summer Tomato Cruda, 95

Mini Grilled Polenta Sandwich, 21–22

One-Pan Pasta Rustica, 147

Roasted Tomato, White Bean, and Spinach Soup, 77

Shrimp Tarte Tatin with Roasted Tomatoes and Calamata Olives, 109

The Steak House Wedge, 32

Summer Tomatoes with Arugula and Steve's Spiced Pecans, 33

Tomato Confit, 66

Tomato-Mozzarella Club with Basil and Balsamic Syrup, 51

Tomato-Poached Shrimp, 20

veal. *See* beef

vegetables. *See* individual vegetables

Vegetable Spoon Explosions, 16

Vermont Maple Crème Brûlée, 117

Warm Spinach with Pan-Roasted Pears and Stilton, 29

Warm Stilton Flan with Grilled Pears and Brown Bread, 39–40

Wild Mushroom and Goat Cheese Tartlets, 52–53

wine, 135–38

zucchini. *See* squash